THE CALL OF THE DRAGON

BEHOLD THE PLEROMA

***

In memory of my father,
Andrew J. Hill, Jr.,
for teaching me transformation.
His wisdom, humor and courage
continue to enhance my personal journey…

~ and ~

In memory of my friend,
Kenneth Rogers,
who I continue to love and miss:
I promise to sing the song of truth and honor—
the sacred message you shared with me.

***

ACKNOWLEDGEMENTS

If I am the ritual leader of Holistic Health Practice, then Sara Davenport is its èminence grise. She has brought integrity and an unmatchable standard of excellence that is the linchpin of our mission. Sara is a quiet leader in our community, and her love and guidance have helped me find the peace and joy necessary to make this book possible. Our spiritual talks have been most enlightening.

My special thanks to Grasshopper (aka Jane Brown Smith). For without her help, this book would not have been published. Through positive regard and encouragement, she provided the thrust I needed to keep going. Her enthusiastic and sensitive attention to story ignited my imagination and offered me a safe space to share more. Thank you, Jane, for taking this remarkable peregrination through time and space with me. How lucky I am to have you in my life.

My son, Kurt A. Hill, Jr., created the artwork for this book. His brilliant imagery and suggested metaphor is astounding. Indeed, if the theory of traducianism were true, Kurt would have inherited all the advanced qualities of our ancestors. Encomiums to you, Kurt, for your inspiring vision and pedagogy.

I so appreciate the enlightened colloquy shared with Tara Sullivan. She is an extraordinary healer who shares her gifts at Holistic Health Practice.

A loving acknowledgement to Regenia Rogers, who taught me reconciliation and showed me the brilliance of forgiveness. Her kindness, love and faith helped save my life.

Enormous thanks to my dear friends who helped me survive one of my most traumatic years: Ken and Virginia Selle, Laura Tesch, Kevin McGirr, Laura Sherman and Sara Davenport.

Thank you to Virginia Clarke for showing me what courage looks like.

My gratitude to those who participated in reading this manuscript before it was published; and to Ginni Selle for her very helpful suggestions.

Special recognition to all at Holistic Health Practice—a community of enlightened healers.

~ Kurt Hill
December 2013

CONTENTS

FOREWORD
by
Jane (Brown) Smith

"The sun doesn't shine because it's dark.
It shines because it's the sun."

~ Kurt Hill

I had the great fortune of hearing about a Chicago-based man who was helping people in profound ways at a time when I had no idea just how much help I needed.

"Kurt Hill" was the name given to me by my friend who had been experiencing mysterious energetic disturbances that were seriously affecting her on a physical level (she had even lost her sense of smell). This friend and I had engaged in shamanism; yet, so far, the healers we knew were unable to help her.

My friend said she felt hopeful when she learned that Kurt, who had reportedly restored life to a powerful indigenous healer in Mexico, was accessible and available to offer her a distance healing session.

I smiled one of the biggest smiles ever when my classmate called to say that after connecting with Kurt by telephone, the disturbing issues she had been experiencing had completely disappeared. Her sense of smell had returned and she was elated!

I was intrigued to say the least. I reached out and felt surprised and delighted when I received a personal e-mail response from Kurt. He expressed such care and a genuine interest in helping. That night, I had what Carl Jung refers to as a "big dream." I knew then that life as I knew it would change and it had everything to do with this gifted man named Kurt Hill.

Kurt has stick-with-it-ness, and that is what has saved me through some very dark times. He doesn't offer his gifts to just a select few—he offers them to each and every Being who sincerely makes a request for assistance.

Through the years, I have found myself scratching my head wondering how Kurt could possibly be this big a container. It just doesn't seem humanly possible! When I ask him, he just smiles his gorgeous light-up-an-entire-room smile and says in his one-of-a-kind healing voice, "I think I'll keep my day job."

What you hold in your hand is more than words written on paper. This manuscript delivers a beneficial vibration that will change you. When I first read Kurt's manuscript, I wept. Through his big compassionate heart and with the steady intention of helping others, Kurt makes himself extraordinarily vulnerable in this book by courageously baring some of his deepest wounds.

This book moved enormous amounts of energy in me. I predict that it will do the same for you; and I wish you the very, very best on your journey …

PREFACE
by Moe Ross, CEO
Sterling Life Productions

Kurt and I have many conversations imbedded in the landscape of our interiors. I hear him in the wind. I hear him in my breath. I see him in the light fog over the meadow and in the center of the hollyhock making its way up the trellis. We haven't always trusted each other in fullness. That's something that takes time, which we have for each other. We met in that window of time when God's hand was fiercely separating and connecting. We were connected to set each other, and others, on fire. We burned each other up. And we torched the shadow of the confused seeker who claimed he was Jesus so he wouldn't have to do the real work. We knew we each must do the work and there are no short-cuts. We both wanted short-cuts ourselves, but we knew. We paid our dues as we journeyed together and swallowed the fire. We were brought together to do the only thing we could do......help.

There's no need for you to try to understand. Kurt Hill is not one to be understood. If you try to understand what is happening in his presence, or when you are riding down the elevator after spending time with him, I promise you that you will touch the hot stove of confusion and you will spin into living hell. Real healers like Kurt are not to be understood with the mind. Real healers have access to "the more" outside of the five sensory worlds. Real healers are tricksters and Kurt Hill is a trickster in the grand scale. He knows how to penetrate the light into the appearance of the demons and what may look like a snake to you, is a rope to him. You will enter his presence wanting and longing for "the more." And you will leave less, so you can have access to more. There will be less of you and you and you so that your life is not always about you. Who you are won't matter to Kurt Hill. He wants you to know THAT you are.

His presence is not for the timid who want to hide out in the illusions we create for safety. He will know the shadow you are carrying. You may want to expose it first to appear aware. But it won't be long until you realize he doesn't need to dwell on your shadow or what you have and have not done in your life. He cares about your light, your sincerity, your heart. The shadows will surface and dance like wild demons in his presence. He may help you put them into the solid walking ground of your life if that is what is best for you. Or he may give your shadows to another era, another lifetime or the angelic realm. You are likely to try to follow and figure it out and do anything to be around him. And if you are wise, you will. You will know he has integrity. You will feel the intent and the love.

The price of admission to be with the trickster Kurt Hill at the grand level is your mind. He will blow your mind. You won't be able to imagine what is going to happen in the magnitude of his presence. What I can tell you for sure is that once your mind is blown, he won't tell you that he is the master of your mind. He will walk by your side as you find **your** way. He won't give you new mental constructs to just create yet another illusion. Kurt Hill is the real deal. He has paid his dues and he wants you to pay yours too. He will want you to move forward in your own evolutionary cycle and he will want you to give back for the common good.

You will know the healers not only by their healings, but also by their humility. Certainly one example of his humility is this story. Kurt didn't tell the world until he was "ordered" from the interior landscape. Kurt is not one to boast. His big word/vocabulary comes from a galaxy consciousness. Don't be fooled into thinking you can't digest this story. Kurt will tell you, and all of us, that you can do as he did and more. And you can. Love is available to all of us.

DREAMS

All night
the dark buds of dreams
open
richly.

In the center
of every petal
is a letter,
and you imagine
if you could only remember
and string them all together
they would spell the answer.

It is a long night,
and not an easy one—
you have so many branches,
and there are diversions—
birds that come and go,
the black fox that lies down
to sleep beneath you,
the moon staring
with her bone-white eye.

Finally you have spent
all the energy you can
and you drag from the ground
the muddy skirt of your roots
and leap awake
with two or three syllables
like water in your mouth
and a sense
of loss—a memory
not yet of a word,
certainly not yet the answer—

only how it feels
when deep in the tree
all the locks click open,
and the fire surges through the wood,
and the blossoms blossom.

~ Mary Oliver

***

Her name was Louise Blache. She never wore shoes and her lambent smile could light up your world. Her glow was so incredible that it was years before I realized she did not have teeth. She smiled from her soul and made me feel warm and welcome. She was a heart with a body built around it. Her stature was enormous. She stood about 5'6" tall and weighed perhaps more than the norm; however, she was perfectly Louise. She was robust yet gentile, powerful but at the same time loving. She reminded me of what Mother Earth must be like. She was my Grandmother Blache.

About 12 years ago a psychic woman asked me who was instrumental in assisting me in my intuitive growth. She said that for some reason she just had to know. Before I could answer, she offered this reading:

I see you sitting on some front porch steps in a place other than Chicago. The steps are red and the house seems to be peach or something. There are oyster shells and plants everywhere. There is an old, stately yet handsome, woman gardening while you and another young boy about six or seven watch her as you eat a chocolate ice cream bar.

16

It is a very hot day. You, and who appears to be your brother, are very happy to be in this quadrangle with this very powerful woman. She loves you two very much. I think this place is in Louisiana. She is so filled with joy. I see a curious look on her face as she questions you about her two dogs which don't seem to be around. You answer her, laughing hysterically, as you tell her that they are hiding under the house. She asks you why and you share with her that they know they are in trouble. She doesn't understand, so you explain to her that they remember you said if they caused her sheets to fall onto the muddy ground again you were going to skin them alive.

This appears to be your grandmother and she was a domestic and did wash for a number of homes. As was customary for people in the sunny south, she used a line to hang things rather than place them in a dryer. They smelled so much fresher.

She loved her work and took pride in helping people. After hearing your tale, she walked over to the garden fence which was a structure of about six feet in height and five-feet wide. She literally had to hold onto the top portion of the gate in order to pull herself up so that she could see if your story was true.

She had this large straw hat on that she wore to protect her from the hot sun. She pushed it back a bit so she would not have trouble seeing. The trowel that she held in her right hand was now placed in her apron. I can see the grimace on her face as she turns to you and asks how you knew that this had happened. She said that a boy your size was not tall

17

enough to see over the fence so how could you know what happened.

The garden fence was a solid gray wood structure with holly all around it. I see that you are telling her that you got the information from the dogs. "Blackie and Whitie told me. Yep, and they know they are in trouble." Your Grandmother Blache just stared at you and said, "So it's you." You immediately retorted that you had nothing to do with it. She smiled and said that she was not blaming you but that she was realizing something for the first time.

"It was you. You have a gift. You see Kurtie Kurt, not everyone can hear animals talk." I see that with a kind stroke of your head and a warm smile she escorted you around the garden and said to you that very day that there was much you need to learn about how to live in this world with the vision you have. She then held both of your shoulders and told you that she understood because she had the gift as well. "Kurtie, you are not alone."

Now, years later, I realize that I use that phrase in my business all the time. "You are not alone." I learned so much from Louise Blache. She accompanies me in much of my healing work. There are just so many wonderful stories and sayings associated with her. "Kurtie Kurt, just pud it in da zink." I loved when it was time to sleep and she would tell me it is time to make "Fe doh doh." She was a sensitive who was steeped in sagacity. Hers was an ancient wisdom that comes from the trees. I could just hang on her branches and listen to her susurrations all day. She had a way!

In 1970, when I was with WVUE television station, I was on a particular show to interview someone. My attitude – as I tell it – was not the best in that I was dealing with a very prejudice person. Because I knew he was limited in his vocabulary and lacked in academic prowess I began to demean him by forcing him into unfamiliar, scholarly zones. I made it clear that I was a sesquipedalian and that he was beneath me on all measurable scales. Yet, he considered himself superior. I was not kind. At one point while I basked in my arrogance, I thought of my Grandmother Blache and remembered that she was watching this program. I also remembered I was going to see her the next day and – like the dogs who were responsible for her muddy sheets – I knew I was in trouble!

The next day I visited her at her house at 1357 Columbus St. in New Orleans. Before I knocked on the door, I began preparing my defense for the demeaning I had done when she appeared at the door. I was determined that she was not going to admonish me. Oh no! I was not going to let her get the jump on me. After all, I was trained to give interviews. I knew how to lead a person into verbal directions. Well, when she came to the door she was wearing one of those very large and colorful garden hats she loved to wear when she was gardening. She gave me a kiss and handed me the most absurd hat one could ever imagine. I explained to her that I just could not wear that outrageous thing. "What if my constituents see me in this?" She smiled and said, "It's just a hat. If you don't cover your head you cannot come into the garden with me because you are going to get a bad sunburn. Hmm Che, don't you know a *free* person could wear this without

19

concern?" I took the hat and proceeded to the place where she and I would spend time and talk. I loved spending time with her. I had helped her in the garden since I was a kid. This was so natural and fun. Yet, I was preparing just how I was going to control the conversation. She was not going to get me this time. So, just before we came to the area where she had beautiful roses, I launched my verbal query. "Mother Blache," I said, "If you could be any age you wanted to be what age would that be?" My grandmother was at least 85 now and had moved out of her favorite home with the garden in the quadrangle of New Orleans. The school district had forced her out because they needed the property to build a new school. I will never forget the day she received the information. Unfortunately, I was told the sad news by a neighbor. "Vinnie ca, vinnie ca, lil Blache. Yo Mau Mau know dat dey gone take all de houses in de neighborhood? What she tink about dat?" Then she said, "Run see what she sey."

I will never forget the hurt on my Grandmother's face. I had never seen her eyes water before in this way. It looked like the mist from the Mississippi river. She placed her warm, large hand on my shoulder and said, "She must be coocoo. Let me go say something to her and then I will go make groceries."

Well, when she returned she looked as if she had been drenched in Dixie Beer. Her face was expressionless. Her heart was broken. She loved that house. Her garden was special. As she lifted her eyelids, revealing a dim glow where before there had been a lambent flare, she said "God is able."

This garden was never going to be the same. Grandmother Blache's garden was like my athletic ability (the older I got the better I was!). Yet, this garden had a personality of its own. Each flower sat up straight as she approached it as though she were a couture preparing someone for grooming. Disney couldn't have drawn her any better. She was my Chocolate Angel. She had a trowel for a wand and she got joy and love all over everything.

Well, anyway, as she was about to answer my age-related question she pushed back her large hat just as she always had. She put her right foot out in front of the other and placed her trowel hand on her hip. "Ha ha I have her now," I thought. She then asked me if I meant older or younger. She was already elderly, so I said "younger." Then she said, "I tink I would want to be dat young goil of 56." I said, "What? 56?" She looked at me and asked, "You asked me da question yeah?" I responded, "Yes, but…" She chuckled and said, "What do you know, che. You don have de turty yeahs on de planet." Then she shared with me this amazing wisdom: "Kurty Kurt, when you are in yo twenties you just an apprentice adult. You spend years of yo life trying to find out who you are. Then you turn turty. You spend 10 years of yo life trying to dig yo self out of all the problems you got yo self in when you were in yo twenties. Den come da forties. You gone look in de mirra and say – das not me, dis is me. So you spend 10 more yeahs trying to figga out which is which. But den 50 come and you gone say dat I don know where I am going but I sho know where I been. You got history with yo self, boy. Den you live five, six mo yeahs and you realize that you are feeling pretty good. You say to yoself that you feelin good and fit. By now you have lost friends and loved ones and you done decide who gone stay in yo life now. No mo aggravating people. Dis time belong to me, laud. Come 56 you feelin strong, good and fit, you done forgot about which age is which. You just lean intah you and be yoself. You take the first breath into you dat ya evah do took che. It gone feel so good. Whew! Happy gone stay with you fo sometime now. You gone want to grow life in everyway you can think about. You are finally free. Free is young. By the time 60 come around you are coasting pretty good just being you. You not gone worry about what age you becoming. You just interested in livin it real and thankin the laud fo each and every day. Dat is why it is so important not to let anyone lead you down a path that is not yoahs. You know, da way you let dat man de odda night do you on the TV."

I could not believe my ears. She had segued into the situation I was trying to avoid. I had been educated and admonished at the same time. She was truly a master teacher. But most of all, I knew she was right. I had lowered my standard in order to strike back at prejudice. I could have held a space of integrity. Instead, I took a short cut and she straightened me like one of her bent flowers. "If you gone be in my garden you got to grow right."

Years later, someone asked me if that story was true. I just smiled and said, "She was a legend. Are legends true?" Then I just continued what I was doing with a knowing smile. If someone were to ask me today, I would simply say that she was my very special Grandmother and I have a number of incredulous stories about her.

Grandmother Blache is who taught me to be aware of the "Dragon." "He's out dare watchin you. He done take the shape of all sorts of things. All bigger dan you, boy. You got to know God is able. You got to know when something is too big to explain. Da Dragon look like he want to go left and he go right. He do a second line in da sky. Sometimes he seem bad and sometimes he seem good and den times he just is. He represents pure potential. Attitude molds tings. Ya nevah know what it gonna du. It's all around. Yet, it styles itself in the manner you need. All of a sudden you look around and you say to yoself dat ya know what ya know and ya know it's near. You heah me?"

I heard her loud and clear.

After my Grandmother died, I did not speak of metaphysical things. In fact, I dedicated my life to disproving psychic phenomenon. I read every book that Carl Sagan wrote in order to disprove that which I knew inside of me. Yet, I could not quench the insatiable fire of knowledge about the "way" that was etched into my being. The more I tried to disprove psychic phenomenon, the more I found evidence to convince me that Sagan was wrong. There are things beyond our reason. My ancestors were obviously talking to me. Tergiversation was not an option here. I must come to know this Dragon. I must begin the journey.

I cannot really say I was aware of the Dragon of which my Grandmother spoke until much later in my life. I chuckle now as I remember how she explained it, this Dragon, doing a second line in the sky. Therefore, I must tell you a story. I must share

23

with you an event that changed my life forever. Hey, Grandmother Blache, you are right—God is able!

***

"That which has no form has no being."

~ Paul Tillich

THE CALL

"If there are only rafts
and these rafts are really language itself,
what is this sea that is 'outside' language
because it is beyond the raft?
Maybe there is no sea either?
If there is only language,
then God must be either
inside language and in that case an idol;
or he is outside language
and there is nothing out there but silence.
There is only one possibility left,
and that is what we can experience
in the movement of the raft,
in the breaks in the raft's structure,
and above all, what can be experienced
at the edges of the raft itself.
For we cannot really talk of the sea,
we can only talk of the edges of the raft
and what happens there.
Our prayer will have to be not
'Thank God for edges' but 'Thank edges for God.'"

~ John Dominic Crossan

***

It was the spring of the year 2000. It was an
unusually busy time for me as I was overwhelmed
with a new phase of my practice. I had just
expanded and decided to offer a number of different
treatments that were non-conventional to the main-
stream medical world. Some might claim that I had

started working with aspects of a powerful magic. Most, in the medical community, had not heard of thaumaturgy and certainly did not want to probe or explore anything outside of an acceptable, modern model of treatment and care.

Yet people of all ages, races and walks of life were seeking help beyond what the allopathic treatment could offer. They were asking questions about energy and phenomenon. Some talked about a deep sense of knowing that their physician was not correct with regard to the terminal illness they had. "There is a cause that my ego seems to be adumbrating," was inculcated by each and every patient who came to me for help. I was being asked to journey with them beyond what had already been discovered.

Nonetheless, as confident as I could be in these kinds of situations, I felt as if there was some sort of training taking place for me as well. It was as if I was being prepared for something beyond my understanding. I was being challenged to exceed my existing realm of possibility and to step into an area where the ego dare not go.

My higher self was placing me in touch with my causal self, as Ken Wilbur would suggest. I knew that I was being called out by the Dragon and could not control its mist surrounding me. This was more than the effluvium that Teilhard De Chardin speaks of in his book, *The Phenomenon of Man*. My intuition warned me that this might be the breath of the real Dragon and, if so, I should beware to check my arrogance at the door.

Modern scholars and practitioners think that the Dragon can be treated like a hand-held puppet; further, that the ego places its hand in the puppet and then uses aggressive forms of onomatopoeia to simulate this mighty form in a falsely safe environment. Certainly this wakes up the imagination and sparks some safe fear in the hearts of those who witness this mockery.

This Dragon was no toy; this was beyond comprehension. Those sequestered in the "Royal" area of Wilbur's quadrants would not allow their perspicacity to reveal the truth about this realm. Yet the "Magician" knows that it is time; it is a time for anagogic reflection and prayer.

According to Robert Moore, the "Magician" knows that he cannot engage this power alone; he knows that the Dragon cannot be domesticated or anthropomorphized, but it can be personalized. The "Royals" will tell you that if you cannot see it, then it must not be there. Besides, there are "Warriors" ready to confront this creature if need be. They are apodictic in their epiplexis, but trust me when I tell you it can see you even when you cannot see it. Like an enthymeme that you think you have an understanding of, but it is still not clear. The Dragon lurks!

So, when the knock came on the door, I was prepared to witness the sequence of events that would come my way. Thoughts regarding the protasis and apodosis did a terpsichore through my brain. I am sure this was just some measure to keep my wits about me. The hairs on the back of my neck stood at attention. Yet, I welcomed my next client in as if I were the "Lover," with no regard for danger or alarm. Even though this was no ordinary client, I postured myself as if I was trained for anything and everything. The truth is, my anxiety level was extreme. This person was definitely a "Trickster" and was ready for the game. But why? With this question to myself, I had an epiphany: I was being prepared for a journey to a terra incognita. Equally, I accepted that I needed to be challenged and groomed for where I was going to be asked to go and what I was about to deal with. My skill set needed to be upgraded and Spirit was giving me the lesson I needed.

During the course of my interaction with this client, he blurted out something about his grandfather who was a shaman. He spoke of incantations and bizarre occurrences that seemed ostensibly to frighten him. What I later learned was that he actually enjoyed the chaos and mysticism. It made him feel special. He truly wanted to be a sorcerer. He thrived on evil and needed to be inflated. He was clever, but not intelligent.

In order to deal with him I had to reach into my quiet knowing and just hold a space of light and knowing. The transformation he was requesting was really a trick. What he wanted was to be in my presence so that he could exsanguinate me of my energy force. He wanted my Chi. But the voice inside my head cautioned me not to allow myself to be roiled by his execrable demeanor. "Stay calm and hold the container" were the words presented to me in my head in a tautological fashion. The voice was mellifluous and reassuring. My anxiety level began to return to normal as I discovered what was really sitting in front of me.

"Let your vibration increase by connecting to your Ultimate of Ultimate Concerns" rang even louder in my head. "Tell your ego to quiet itself" was the hardest advice for me. I wanted to demonstrate my talent and skill as a great healer and holistic practitioner. I wanted to awaken my Warrior, but this was not a battle a soldier could know anything about. It felt as if I were in another dimension. My Self knew and coerced me to listen to the soothing voice within.

It was as if antiphons filled the room along with tones of joy which vibrated from my being. It was at this point the client could no longer stand being in my presence; he yelled as though he was trying to distract me. He resisted the healing that he said he wanted and needed and, after projecting a loud, ignominious expletive, he left screaming that he had been exposed.

Needless to say, my nerves were on end. However, I kept my eyes closed and listened to another calming voice from within. It was at that time that I knew something else was near.

"Past, present and future exist simultaneously. Time is just an historical manifestation of existence. You are already there waiting for yourself to show up. Your reality may not be authentic." These were phrases from sages past that sang out like a chorus to me while I was trying to step back into a realm of meaningful behavior. Lawrence LeShan would say that I had just experienced the world of the paranormal. The anatomical code in me was being confronted by a strange new world; an environment that had a different coding (Stevens).

The call to action was not an exigent one, but I felt I should do something such as tell someone of this happening, or write it down and ask myself if it really happened. Perhaps a primal scream would do. I realized that I had been coerced to step outside my familiar and I could not return to my old paradigm again. My ego had been introduced to the Self, and I had survived this first of many rounds.

The client was simply a player in this magical drama. I had an appointment with destiny that was apparently sine die. Everything I was encountering was a mere succedaneum for my encounter with Dragon. What other way to take a prerequisite for such a venture?

More days slowly went by while I waited for my marching orders. When nothing came, I thought maybe I was the victim of an over-active imagination. Had I read too many books about phenomenon? I was beginning to believe I actually did have abilities beyond the average individual. I was beginning to language myself back into a more familiar realm and re-entry was grounding me in a manner that would not help me later.

That's when it happened: she contacted me with a sense of urgency. Dr. Casey Carter used her professional, medical voice all the while pleading me to take a strange and unusual journey with her into the Sierra Madre mountains of Mexico in order to save a life. She said a particular shaman had seen me in a dream, and she knew that it was me who was needed. She said he had seen others, but they were modern shamans and had no real respect for the magic. I asked her just who she thought I was! I could hear the smile over the phone. She said she wanted me to think on it and that she would contact me later the next day.

Call it antonomasia or whatever; that night I dreamed about someone who answered to the name of Wolf or Wolf Man. As I continued to dream, I followed the man as he changed from time to time into a wolf and then back into a man. He was definitely a shape shifter and he was beckoning me. He kept waving his hand toward himself in order to get me to come his way. I felt myself acknowledge him and then I abruptly woke up. It felt like I had been in some sort of tropical place and it was as if I had sand on my feet. I had not been out of my bed though. I was uneasy because I was wrestling with an unbelievable schedule and reasoning with myself as to just why I could not travel to see this shaman. It just was not practical. Perhaps he could be sent to me in Chicago and I could work with him there? I was still curious about the dream.

I am certain that Casey must have been acting as a vicegerent for the shaman because the doctor persisted with her pleas, "you must, you must" she kept saying. I was recalcitrant but I could feel myself weakening.

That night I had another dream: I could see a tribe off in the distance and a priest or minister who was quietly purporting his views about mystigogical catechesis. It was as though he was teaching this tribe about the ancient and mystical ways of their religion. Then the wolf came in my view and I woke up out of this very deep sleep. At least I think it was a sleep! It felt like I was there standing with this man who was held in such esteem by his tribe. The people of this autochthonous antediluvian tribe seemed to be referring to him in a hagiographical manner. They were ululating as though this was some kind of ritual purging. The priest had an inveterate disposition about his procedure and would not let anything distract him. No one seemed concerned about preterition. There was a sublime confidence that this ritual leader had everything under control. I heard myself ask, "who is this man?"

That same day, Casey contacted me again. I had already decided to say no. I could not leave my practice. This just did not seem feasible. I immediately envisioned the wolf again and the phone rang simultaneously. Casey continued with her remonstrating about the need for me to go, even though my appointment calendar was already filled to the end of the year. She did not let that distract her. She said she felt it was the right thing to do. At last, she agreed to stop contacting me about the matter and to respect my decision.

The rest of the day was all about renascence. The people, the plants, me—we all needed to be rejuvenated. It was as if the world was confabulating with me. I sat down at my desk and began to meditate before I saw my next client. To my surprise, my next client was in my head. I could see this man in the dream reaching out to me for help while warning me to be careful. I was moved with compassion and love. I knew I had to find this soul and assist him.

When I called Casey, she had already purchased my ticket. I laughed and then asked her about my accommodations. After she told me she was going to go with me, she said that we were going to stay with the Huichol Indians. I inquired about the living conditions and she told me not to worry. "It's not the Holiday Inn, but it is livable."

I could not believe what I was about to do; but I knew I had to go. In fact, I was already there. I could feel it in my bones. I could also feel the room change. Something was hot and I could sense the Dragon's nostrils close to my right ear. With my heart palpitating as though it was doing trance drumming, I turned to look but to no avail. The Dragon was palpable but still invisible.

While I prepared for this excursion, I wondered what had happened to this man. I was now calling him a shaman because my friend had told me that he was quite renowned. He was the ritual leader of this tribe, and he was well known in Arizona and California by the alternative medical community. He was something of a legend. Hmmmm . . . a shaman. A shaman and he has need of my help? I could not imagine what he would require. What I did know was that I had to show up with piety and humility. I could not be arrogant in any way, shape, fashion or form. The Westerner stance was not going to be allowed on the premises. Although I did not know what was expected of me, I somehow felt I already knew this man.

Edward Edinger might say that I was experiencing the transference of phenomenon or an encounter with the greater personality. In his book, *Science of the Soul,* he writes:

> The basic question concerning the relation of the personal to the archetypal in psychological development is this: to what extent is personality development determined by innate, a priori patterns within the individual – namely, the *archetypal factor* – and to what extent is it determined by personal experience and influence from environment, cultural forms and significant personal relationships – the *personal factors*? (61).

This author is plugged into a larger-than-life scenario. He was channeling the archetypal father energy. Upon this realization, everything started to spin and the voice told me to be still in my center for awhile. There I would find a place of nothingness and that I was to remember that nothing is either good or bad, but thinking makes it so.

I began to think about the training I had in structural cognitive modifiability. Then the room began to disappear and I was calm again but cold. What was the coldness that I felt? Death…is that you?

In a lecture, Edinger said:

> …the basic feature of Jungian psychology – the ego and how it relates to the reality of the Self. Jungian psychology is the only psychological standpoint that operates out of an

awareness that there are two centers in the psyche. Some other psychologies, some other analytic approaches, have an awareness that there are two entities in the psyche; there is an unconscious and there is a second entity. But no other psychological standpoint operates out of the awareness that there are two 'centers'. That is unique to Jungian psychology. And since there are two centers, if that comes to conscious realization, then those two centers must collide, they must have an encounter with each other. That happens when the ego, which is the little center, has an encounter with the Self, the big center.

All psychological analysis is no more than a prelude to this experience, the encounter with the Self. Here is how Jung put it: "Analysis should release an experience that grips us or falls upon us from above, an experience that has substance and body such as those things which occurred to the ancients. If I were going to symbolize it, I would choose the Annunciation."

Now, it may very well happen that this crucial experience, although it is prepared for by analysis, does not take place during the period of regular analysis at all. It may take place many years later.

It is equally important here to note the meaning of enantiodromia. Enantiodromia is a concept introduced by psychiatrist Carl Jung where the superabundance of any force inevitably produces its opposite. It is equivalent to the principle of equilibrium in the natural world, in that any extreme is opposed by the system in order to restore balance. Jung used it to refer to the unconscious acting against the wishes of the conscious mind. Enantiodromia literally means "running counter to," referring to the emergence of unconscious opposite in the course of time. This characteristic phenomenon practically always occurs when an extreme, one-sided tendency dominates conscious life and, in time, an equally powerful counter-position is built up (which first inhibits the conscious performance and subsequently breaks through the conscious control).

I will use this term as a neoplasm to describe the tendency of the younger generation to manifest the undesirable traits of a previous generation, despite the repudiation of these traits when they were young. I am referring here to the Huichol Indian tribe. Here I am borrowing from the concept of John Calvin as well (as it is depicted in the *Institutions*).

Now a syzygy is being formed. The shaman, the tribe, and I are beginning to take shape in this drama. I am thinking about this as I board the plane in order to meet my friend so that I can start the journey to Mexico. Am I alone?

As the crowded plane began to touch down, I realized I had been asleep. I am not certain because it felt as though I had done some remote viewing. I did not feel I was centered in my body. As I began to settle myself, I reflected just a little about my dream. It was the shaman changing into a wolf. This time I was sure. My rational mind wanted to rescue

36

me from fantasy. My imagination was running wild.
I needed to step back into meaningful behavior.
None of this made sense. Yes, we have all seen
movies about such things, but they are just
fantasy—right?

Remember that Jung speaks of such in his treatment
of the theriomorphic spirit symbolism in fairytales.
Jung explains in his book, *The Four Archetypes:*

> The description of our archetype would
> not be complete if we omitted to
> consider one special form of its
> manifestation, namely its animal form.
> This belongs essentially to the
> theriomorphism of gods and demons
> and has the same psychological
> significance. The animal form shows
> that the contents and functions in
> question are still in the extrahuman
> sphere, i.e., on a plane beyond human
> consciousness, and consequently have a
> share on the one hand in the
> daemonically superhuman and on the
> other in the bestially subhuman. It must
> be remembered, however, that this
> division is only true within the sphere of
> consciousness, where it is a necessary
> condition of thought. Logic says *tertium
> non datur,* meaning that we cannot
> envisage the opposites in their oneness.
> In other words, while the abolition of an
> obstinate antinomy can be no more than
> a postulate for us, this is by no means so
> for the unconscious, whose contents are
> without exception paradoxical or
> antinomial by nature, not excluding the
> category of being. If anyone
> unacquainted with the psychology of the

> unconscious wants to get a working
> knowledge of these matters, I would
> recommend a study of Christian
> mysticism and the Indian philosophy,
> where he will find the clearest
> elaboration of the antinomies of the
> unconscious (128).

So, you can rationalize anything, right? And as quoted in LeShan's book, *The World of the Paranormal* (as he discusses space, time, and paranormal events), he refers to the physicist, Pascual Jordan, who points out the importance of a condition of parapsychology. He states that we must change our conception of space in our work:

> We must adopt a radically different
> attitude, remembering that three-
> dimensional space, as we usually
> conceive it, is not an immediate
> experience, but the result of prior work
> by our mind and prior condition of what
> we may observe (qtd. in Jung "Four
> Archetypes" 95).

So now I am ex-cogitating in order to make certain that I am not hallucinating. I didn't even realize that I had left the plane and was standing in front of my friend. She didn't say hello. She stared at me and said, "Ready?" There was something different about me. I was in a state of preparation. You know, like a priest who is ready and waiting to celebrate the mass. He knows the full value of what he is about to undertake and he is transformed for the task. As we boarded the plane and took our seats in the middle of the plane, she turned to me and finally said his name: "Don Lupe." I repeated it, and then it dawned on me: well of course that's his name! "Don Lupe" is a name that signifies man and wolf.

Without committing blasphemy, I thought of Calvin's arguments in the Institution about the significance of the sacrament of communion. Albeit Calvin does not believe the transformation takes place, he is very vehement about the signifier, the sign, and the significance of the sacrament.

Transformation? Don Lupe was the shaman who came to me in my dream. Don Lupe was the theriomorphic being that kept contacting me in the shape of a wolf. How is this possible and did this really happen? Maybe I am just having the "big dream" Jung talks about. And then the voice returned. It floated through the aisles of the plane like the susurration of the wind, chanting quieting notes that had a soporific effect on me.

I was not wanting to be rude, but I was completely ignoring my friend. I was caught up in my own world—or the shaman's. Just as I was about to close my eyes I thought I saw something flying next to the right wing of the plane. The sun was reflecting off the very-red left eye of this creature. It was watching me. I know it. Why didn't anyone else seem disturbed by its presence? It was the size of the plane and its face appeared to resemble a chimera I once saw in a small town in Europe. As much as I did not want to determine this, I did have to acknowledge it. No … it couldn't be …was this a mantichora?

In his book, *The Secret Teachings of All Ages*, Manly P. Hall describes the mantichora as the most remarkable of allegorical creatures:

> …the *mantichora*, which Ctesias describes as having a flame-colored body, lionlike in shape, three rows of teeth, a human head and ears, blue eyes, a tail ending in a series of spikes and

stings, thorny and scorpionlike, and a voice which sounded like the blare of trumpets. This synthetic quadruped ambled into medieval works on natural history, but, though seriously considered, had never been seen, because it inhabited inaccessible regions and consequently was difficult to locate (265).

This was not exactly a man's face, and I almost shouted to the other passengers: "Look out! It's going to breathe fire!" I had never seen a dragon before and, when sleep came, there was darkness.

When we arrived in Mexico we were hustled off in a jeep with the guide who was going to accompany us into the region. He wanted us to know that no one around these parts ever goes up there: "They are an isolated people; the government will not assist you if you get into trouble; and they really do not like strangers." He wanted to know if I was completely out of my mind: "Do you really think that you can achieve what you are here to do? Have you considered the consequences if you fail?"

In Robert Moore's book, *Facing the Dragon – Confronting Personal and Spiritual Grandiosity*, he informs:

> Your unconscious grandiosity still functions beneath your repression, but you regulate it through the psychological prosthesis of splitting it off onto the group. This psychological tactic enables you to function more or less normally and appear more psychologically developed than you really are. Without such a prosthesis

40

you would have to face the dragon
consciously and either continue
consciously the processes of
individuation or become psychotic.

A person in a group can say, "This
group is a new cult, and everyone
outside it is doomed, but me personally,
I'm humble, and I'm just doing what
God wants me to do."

In the context of this social group, I am
humble, and so are all my fellow
members. Everyone in the group is
humble. We can be humble precisely
because we belong to a group that has
the only tickets available for seats on
the great cosmic spaceship that is just
about to come.

He continues:

Regulating grandiosity is a universal
human need, because everyone has to
deal with this same great dragon within.
We are not are not stupid. We have an
inner magician, an inner magus, our
Merlin or Gandalf, whispering in our
ear, saying, "Robert, if you get any
more great, you're moving toward a
severe psychosis, so you need to get a
bigger vessel for your grandiosity"
(158).

As the jeep was steered on a back road with no
light, and on a night that was pitch black, I kept
thinking about what the guide said. I could tell he
thought I was arrogant. In fact, who did *I* think I
was? Was I dealing with apotheosis? Why wasn't I

41

carrying an apotropaic medal of some kind? What was this strange feeling of power I was feeling? What am I really about to meet?

I suddenly realized that I was not prepared for this; I had not done any kind of stewardship. I was being grandiose. Then I heard the voice in my head again tell me to be still and remember that I was called here. The guide then yelled, "What was that? Did you feel that burst of wind as though it came from a giant wing?"

It had to have been about three o'clock in the morning when we finally pulled into this desolate village. It was unusually cold and damp. Something was howling with an intention of letting the inhabitants know that a stranger had arrived. It didn't seem real. There was a strange mist all around us. All I wanted to do was go to my room and sleep for a year. I was so tired from the trip. "This is just not me … I am energized on trips. What is going on? Can't anyone get that howling animal to shut up?"

A hand came out of nowhere and fell on my shoulder. It was Casey saying that there was no time to rest. I was needed immediately. I was exhausted and had been told I did not have to do any treatment on this man until the next day when the sun was up and I could recharge myself. "You are needed now!"

I am not exaggerating when I tell you that this man who looked to be older than the mountains lay lifeless on a cold, dirty surface in his adobe. The roof of the place was made of grass and there were no modern appliances. The light was from a dimly lit area off to the side. I don't think I have ever seen a bulb like that before. The rest of the area was illuminated by a fuel lamp of some kind. A woman with a face of stone (to whom I was being introduced in Spanish by Casey) was the wife of Don Lupe. Both were without shoes and their feet looked like the hooves of an animal. The skin on this woman was discolored due to the dust on her. Yet, she had a pleasant odor and a kindness in her face. I don't remember if she had teeth. Her eyes were tearful, but joyous. Somehow I just knew that she was the acting shaman, and that I was an anathema to the rest of the villagers. She made no sound as she glanced down at the remains of her husband and sighed. She would not stop staring at me. She looked at me as though she knew me from somewhere. I could swear that she was communicating with the unseen villagers who elected not to join us. They were confined to their cottages. Why?

In another of Robert Moore's books, *The Archetype of Initiation: Sacred Space, Ritual Process, and Personal Transformation*, he discusses the work of Mircea Eliade:

> The historian of religions Mircea Eliade has made important contributions to our understanding of initiation in his many books, especially *The Sacred and the Profane* (1961), *Patterns in Comparative Religion* (1959), and *Rites and Symbols of Initiation* (1958). His basic thesis is that all human space-time is heterogeneous, that is, it exists in two different forms: (a) ordinary profane

space and time which he believes
modern people live in almost all the
time, and (b) sacred space and time that
only tribal, pre-industrial peoples could
access at certain times (90).

I was standing somewhere between these two
worlds. This was not liminal space, which is
between time and space (a place one resides just
before transformation). This was some other realm.
Could this be what Moore calls ludic behavior? I
was in some sort of trance. It was as if the Holy
Spirit had entered the room. My hands were moved
in his direction and I got down on that dirty ground
and merged with that man until I could feel his life
force reignite. It was as if a bolt of lightning hit
him.

His wife began to cry and shout. The doctor was
frozen in her space and I was just a witness. The
room was aglow. God was doing His work and I
was a conduit. Fools Crow was right…the healer is
like a hollow bone; the energy runs through it and
the healer gets the credit. All healers have to do is
keep the bone clean.

When the current stopped, it was daylight. I was
incoherent and do not know why I did not pass out.
The doctor escorted me to my abode. It was an
adobe with a dirt floor and a stale smell of filth. I
could not believe my eyes. My body ached and I
was thirsty. I was not dressed or ready for this
shock. As I fell to the floor the old woman came in
and covered me with a horse blanket that had been
on one of the horses out back (Don Lupe's horse).

The blanket was dusty and rough. For a brief moment I remembered I had asthma.

I felt annoyed because my friend did not tell me the truth about the housing, and I was becoming more irritable when the voice came again. This time I was told to focus on the light. It was beautiful and it had a special shape. I think it was in the shape of a diamond. Trailing off to sleep, I knew that Don Lupe was alive and somehow I thought I remembered his wife coming in my room to tell me, "he lives!" Then I heard the crow of a rooster.

The old woman had placed some sort of symbol on my door. I could hear the voices of natives nearby. I was alone in the adobe even though three of us (Casey, me, and the guide) had been ordered to sleep there. I sat up and realized what had transpired earlier that morning. I was not aware that it was almost three o'clock in the afternoon now and everyone had been up for hours. Don Lupe and I were the only two people in the village who were not yet stirring. "Symbol," I thought. Interesting.

John Weir Perry, M.D. wrote a book titled *The Self in Psychotic Process*. In it he writes about the amplification of the symbol:

> During the past several decades considerable scientific work has been done on the study of the morphology and nature of the symbol of the quadrated circle. All possible sources, from primitive cultures to the most refined, have been examined for examples of any commonly recurring symbols and symbolic processes. In this way, just as with the early researches in

any scientific field, the various phenomena have been found to fall into groups according to their characteristics and functions; that is, the data have been examined impartially, regularities found, and classifications made, such as the symbols of the Hero, the Great Mother, the Divine Child, and the death and rebirth, the quarternity, and the quadrated circle. Similar patterns have been found to occur spontaneously in the material of analysants, and these have been added to the compilation of data.

The use of these studies is two fold. In the direction of the pure science, there has developed an extensive knowledge of symbolic expression and its implications in the evolution of consciousness and culture. In the direction of therapy, this knowledge has proved indispensable for an adequate understanding of the meaning of the various symbols occurring in dreams and fantasies and for an effective use of them. In the latter use, the method for elucidating the meaning of the symbol has been called "amplification," which is the enrichment of the fantasy material by the analogous material of its parallels found in comparative symbolism (39).

The voice returned in my head. This time I could hear the words of St. Bartholomew, "Imagination gives shape, form, and color to unformed mental energy—both positive and negative." I wondered, "Am I imagining all of this? Is this real? Am I in some sort of trance; and what is that strange humming sound outside?"

I got up with the worst pain I ever had in my back. I did not have a restful sleep and when I became conscious of just where I was resting, I wanted to disappear. I felt hot and dirty. I was having trouble living in my body. I needed to get out of the adobe and mingle. I stood up and dusted off. You have no idea how much I abhor being dirty and disheveled! "There won't be a good sartorial statement made by me today," I grumbled. I was a giant wrinkle.

There were no mirrors. I was sweating profusely because it had become so very hot. I do not do well in heat. "What is that mephitic odor?" I could not believe my friend had made only these arrangements for my stay here in this primitive place. Yet, it was perfect.

As I stepped out of the hut, I saw Casey standing about 50 yards away from me. She was barefoot and seemingly in her element. She is quite a special doctor. She also stands with a foot in both worlds, simply using a different modality in order to get lift off.

As she started toward me, I noticed numerous scorpions jetting between us. She did not seem concerned about the apparent danger. A sting from one of those could be quite serious; yet, she continued to perambulate in my direction. Although she had a smile on her face, she had the face of a scientist as well.

"Okay, tell me what happened last night and how you did that? And why couldn't I move? Come on, I need S.O.A.P. notes." Then she smiled again and asked me how I was doing. While she continued to question me she followed me like an amanuensis. As I shared, I could not help but notice just how dry and wrinkled the land was. It looked like the tired old face of Don Lupe. I thought, "So that's it; he's a personification of the land. He's holding this container without an interregnum; no wonder this man is exhausted."

Casey persisted. She wanted to know something about what had transformed. "Don Lupe was not alive; he was not breathing and he had all of the signs of a person who had just died. Since I'm a doctor, I just want to know *how*?"

A healer focuses on the source of the light that is shown, often times in the center of the sixth chakra. Receiving the code from that source, the healer proceeds with the healing. The power does not belong to the healer; it belongs to the Ultimate Concern. The healer is merely a conduit. If properly trained, the healer knows not to try to access it from within but to accept it directly from the source itself. Such a power can only be activated with a good and sacred intention, actualizing through the imagination in order to manifest in the third dimension.

The healer must also envision the person as if he or she has already been healed and be willing to hold a sacred space until the connection is made. It is extraordinary and very sacrosanct. The great power is granted by, and delivered from, the Holy Spirit.

No human has the ability to do this level of healing. I am humbled to think that I was allowed to witness this great power. It has changed my life forever.

I need you to know …

Don Lupe emerged from his abode. The villagers had not seen him for more than three months; he was a very sick man. Yet, here he was glowing and smiling and walking with a strut you see from the flambo carriers during Mardi Gras in New Orleans. He was magnificent! I knew he could not wait to meet the man who had helped him. I heard myself thinking, "Well, this is how I should answer when he thanks me and tells me what a wonderful healer I am. I should present myself in a humble manner."

I could feel the excitement running through my being. As I watched him approach me, I could tell that he was acknowledging the people in the village. What a kind soul this man was. He was more than avuncular; he was the town priest or leader.

"What joy!" I thought. "Just think … I am a part of this." When Don Lupe was a least five feet in front of me, he began to utter something. I was still seated because he really had not stopped walking just yet. He passed by me in order to taste some of the wonder food that the women of the village had prepared that morning. Even though he did not study me, I knew he was cognizant of every inch of my body. He lifted his hand in a gesture to acknowledge me and pointedly said, "less food."

What an authentic being he was. He knew that I was not the power. He knew from whence it came. I had never seen such a genuine person. Wonderful!

After he finished eating and drinking, we took a walk. He wanted to show me the land. He spoke to me in guttural sounds like the guttural sounds in Beaulieu's book, *Music and Sound in the Healing Arts*. I understood him clearly. What I missed, Casey translated for me. It was not a Western experience. He held a sacred space with me while we squatted in the grass overlooking the plain and the mountain areas. I could feel the presence of God.

I told him that for some reason the healing was not done. I heard the words come out of my mouth. "Don Lupe, you will be visited by three of your ancestors tonight. You have a choice to make that involves your life. Each are messengers in their own right. I can support you, but I cannot save you. Because you crossed over, you are in touch with something beyond this dimension. If you survive this night, I must construct a sacred circle for you made from the rocks of this great land. I am to perform a ritual ceremony involving you and your people. There is much to do and I have to hold the space for you tonight. Know that this is larger than me. I am so little compared to what sizeable feat I am to face. I am shaken! I want you to know that you are not alone. However, the choice to live or die is near."

Death had beaten me before and left me mangled and humbled. I knew to not be arrogant in the face

of what was to come. I could feel my modernity
shift and I would never practice holistic health the
same. I was being initiated as well. I was shaking,
but resolute.

We continued to sit quietly for the next few hours
until Don Lupe's wife called us for refreshments.
At that point, we stared at each other and shared the
knowing. Right then he looked up and out and I
said to him, "I am sorry, I think I brought it with
me." He said, "Are you sure you did not follow it
here?" I was not surprised, "So you see it too?"

The most amazing and ineffable occurrences were
in store for us in the days to follow. It has taken me
years to write about it. I did not even have the
language until the class I took from Robert Moore
that same year. I could not sum up the events in the
style of a story teller for a tribe without sounding
like it was a peroration. I knew I had to be
authentic. It would be pseudepigraphy to write this
as though it were mine. Don Lupe is the author of
this story. He was writing it. I just had to find the
proper words and expressions.

You are not going to believe the rest of this story. It
changed my life and humbled me forever. The
myth of redemptive violence was shifted in my
thought process as well. I became ashamed of my
arrogance. I knew I needed help. I knew I needed a
place of worship. I knew I needed a higher power.

I know the danger of "psychological feudalism." I
am cognizant of the seduction of grandiosity. This
is beyond my human condition and if I am not
careful and respectful I may have the ultimate

inflation and self destruct. Was this a voice, or the susurration of the wind reminding me to be cautious of infantile transference?

THE HEALING

"Belief is stronger than truth, but the truth will set you free from the limits of belief."

~ Anonymous

***

"To the believer, no proof is necessary
To the non-believer, no proof is possible."

~ Anonymous

***

This was by no means a Potemkin village. Their thoughts and actions were congruent. I was sitting in the center of the truth. I was actually observing past, present, and future existing simultaneously as I sat in front of this incredible fire with my friend, Casey, and our guide.

I continued to ruminate over the task at hand. I was in a trance-like state. Yet, I knew in some way I was communicating with Don Lupe. The flames of the fire grew stronger and crackled with a language that I began to understand. There is no separation here; it is all one. It was time to prepare him for the events to follow. The night had an agenda: energy wanted to express itself in different forms to him, and we were to witness. Although I was not certain as to what that meant, I knew that we were in the center of a potential phenomenon. How he handled the visitation would determine whether or not he would live through the night. His ancestors had every intention of manifesting themselves to him. My surrounding colleagues were cognizant of my inner struggle. They silently supported me with their presence as they fed the fire with more small logs while taking deep breaths and releasing knowledgeable sighs. There was a clear and present danger. We had a task.

I knew it was time to share my visions and inner knowing with Casey. So, we decided to meander about the countryside and talk. We were not prepared for what transpired.

It was a very caliginous and dismal night. As we perambulated through the dimly lit path we could feel how contiguous the creatures of the forest were to us. Even though the animals were camouflaged by the shrubs and foliage, their presence was felt. We became cognizant of the possibility that this path was conterminous with the start of a mystical path.

I felt myself starting to enter into a catechetical dialog with my friend. It felt channeled. I knew she was filled with information and knowledge that began to just pour out of her as well. We were like two waterfalls exchanging information about our watery journey. Both of us were aware of the confluence that had to take place at the bottom of the fall. No, this was not about ego. We were part of the mass of energy we call life. All of the information was present. All we had to do is allow ourselves to be fully present and willing to spill. It was as if we were witnessing ourselves from afar.

Was this some sort of trance? Were we in liminal space and time?

Whatever was happening was certainly extraordinary. Everything seemed to be vibrating and we felt as if we were moving in slow motion. Past, present, and future seemed to be existing simultaneously again. Then we saw it: some sort of cockaigne that had positioned itself right here in this desolate space. Would this be the source of a peripeteia of personal relationships to follow?

I sometimes struggle with the difference between enantiodromia and peripeteia when they are used in certain psychological explanations regarding shifts in paradigms. Was I about to venture into an area of existence known as the Pleroma? Such mystery!

I imagine I should say more about the Pleroma. Here is what I think I know: In his book, *Answer to Job: A Commentary*, Paul Bishop discusses just what the Pleroma is. He states:

> The Nothing, or fullness, is called by us the Pleroma. In it thinking and being cease, because the eternal is without qualities. In it there is no one, for if anyone were, he then would be differentiated from the Pleroma and would possess qualities which would distinguish him from the Pleroma.

> By contrast, the Creatura is the realm of space and time, where everything is individuated, hence individual, including the opposites, which are hence very much not united: The created world is not in the Pleroma, but in itself. The Pleroma is the beginning and the end of the

created world. The Pleroma penetrates the
created world as the sunlight penetrates the air
everywhere. Although the Pleroma penetrates it
completely, the created world has no part of it,
just as an utterly transparent body does not
become either dark or light in colour as the result
of the passage of the light through it. We
ourselves, however, are the Pleroma so it is that
the Pleroma is present within us (61).

Bishop goes on to state that the differentiation is creation;
the created world is indeed differentiated. Differentiation is
the essence of the created world and, for this reason, the
created also causes further differentiation. That is why man
himself is a divider, inasmuch as his essence is also
differentiation.

For a moment we just stood there thinking and watching a
bush in front of us glow in the dark. There was a huge
magenta hue spilling over the area. Amid this, and our
thoughts regarding the magnitude of the Pleroma, I heard
Casey utter, "I think this is what Moses saw when he called
it a burning bush."

As we allowed ourselves to regain consciousness from this
semipiternal event, we suddenly realized that we were
standing in the road in the midst of a stampede! All the
animals of the village were feverishly charging toward us as
if they were frightened by life itself. Yet, I felt invisible and
aware; like we were visiting some extraordinary realm.
Simultaneously, we could hear in the distance a woman
singing. It was a cacophony of sounds. The villagers were
shouting, "Boracha, callete, Boracha, callete." The
metachronal motions seen in the frightened animals were
the only signs of rhythmic beat. The guitar or banjo that a
young, visiting White woman was strumming was creating
a problem for everyone in the village. She seemed to be

oblivious to it all, and that made it even more amusing. The stampede, her lousy singing and playing, and the shouts from the villagers all compiled into a swirling reality of surrealism that caused us to burst into laughter. It was all too much to believe. Miraculously, the animals passed right by us; it was as though we were invisible. We were viewing them from the rear now, and both of us were amazed and in awe of the moment. We then followed the horrible tones of the young woman's country song to the village in order to prepare. This was promising to be an extraordinary night.

Earlier, I had explained to Don Lupe that he was going to be visited by three entities this night. Only then could a decision be made concerning his life or death. They were the "Ancestors" of the tribe. Counsel would send what was needed. Believe me, I had no idea where that information came from at the time when it spilled out of me. Yet, Don Lupe nodded as though he knew exactly what I was talking about and then he went into his hut to prepare for the visitation.

When we returned, not one of the villagers was in sight. It seemed like a ghost town. I noticed an oil light flickering in a camp tent about twenty yards away from the hut where we would be staying that night. I walked over to it and found that the woman we had heard singing earlier was staying there alone. She said she had come in order to be tutored in the ways of a shaman. She wanted instruction from Don Lupe, but when she arrived she realized that he was quite ill. So she decided to just camp and wait. I told her that tonight may prove to be an unusual night. I warned her of the events expected. I told her it might be a better idea to just come in and bunk with the rest of us. She decided not to and I was concerned for her. Although I was cohortative about her quest, I did not think it was wise that she stay out in this wilderness alone and unprotected. Then, somehow I knew it was time for me to return to my hut to prepare.

There were three of us in the hut. My cot was perpendicular to Casey's, and our guide's cot was at a right angle to mine. We were clothed in what we wore the entire day except for our shoes. We knew we needed to sleep because we were quite tired and did not know how long before the bizarre events would occur.

The hut was dirty and dark. It had one little overhead light. There was just a bulb hanging over a refrigerator that seemed to come out of the last century. We had been given patio chairs that could fold into a horizontal position in order for us to sleep. This was not going to be a comfortable night. The temperature continued to drop until it was damp and cold in the hut. I was again covered with the blanket that belonged to Don Lupe's horse. This was definitely not the accommodations my friend had promised, but …

The susurration of the wind sounded like voices apprising us of the danger ahead. I kept reminding myself that it was only wind until our guide's cot started to vibrate and he began to scream in fear. He asked for forgiveness in a way that was unique to the tribe. He said that he had violated the honor of the tribe and that he felt death near him. Tonight was a night of reckoning. At that point, Casey sat up in her cot and tried to calm him. We looked at each other for some logical explanation for his behavior. She said it must be some form of sleep paralysis. I knew of sleep paralysis because of the book written by Paul Chambers titled *Sex and the Paranormal*. The problem with this diagnosis was that he was not paralyzed. He was shaking and shouting and his cot was vibrating in an unusual manner. This was beyond reason and, suddenly, the room became very cold and it seemed as though we had become enveloped in a large shadow. It was as if a giant shadow was standing over our hut! We felt so very small and vulnerable and that is when I thought our guide was going to faint. He pointed to the window and said, "it is here." Reluctant to look, I turned to the window and could not believe what I thought I was witnessing. It was indeed a supernatural, shadow-like entity of some kind. It was ancient and it could crush us at will.

Strangely enough, I was not frightened. For some reason I knew that I had to go outside and build a giant fire. Everything seemed to quake at this point and the sounds around us were intense. This was without a doubt other-worldly. Each of us acknowledged to one another with glares and nods that we were witnessing this something. My friend held the guide and comforted him. She assured him that if it was his time to die, he would be dead. This was a warning for him; he had violated a promise he made to Don Lupe and the villagers. They seemed to know the severity of the oath. Her words did not console or comfort him, and he was beside himself with fear and guilt. His cot began to shake and move back and forth and up and down as though someone was toying with him at will. We were all amazed and thought that he might just die of fear.

I thought about my college days at Xavier University. I was nineteen years of age and had not told my fellow students about my gift of Sight. One evening, a student from downstairs came running to my room, pleading for help, because his bed was vibrating and moving from side to side even though no one was near it. I remember wondering how he knew I was aware of such phenomenon. When I walked into his dark room, the bed was as he had stated; there was a glow around it and the mattress was bending up and down in the middle, as though someone was sitting on it and

59

bouncing up and down. I turned to him and told him that his mother was trying to communicate with him. I felt she had recently died and, after he confirmed that fact, he allowed her to share her thoughts. He cried and said she had died before he could make it home to be by her side. He had a great love for his mother and wanted to be certain she was in a good place. When we could no longer feel her presence in the room, he thanked me as he peacefully sat in an easy chair and asked to be alone. To this day I do not know how he knew that I could help him in this way.

After what seemed like an eternity, the shaking stopped and the guide began to ramble in a litany that he would never violate the ways of his people again. He kept saying that his life would be different now. He felt he had been spared and could not dishonor the spirit that visited him this night. While this was happening, we could hear the howls of dogs; the animals in the village were crying out in protest or prayer. This was an event. We were shivering because the room had become quite cold and damp. We just continued to look at each other to make certain we were not imagining this occurrence. This was the moment I had warned Don Lupe about even though I had no idea what to really expect.

We had settled for about an hour or so when suddenly the room began to swirl and my dear friend's cot began to shift and move as well. She screamed and all three of us pulled our cots together and just huddled. It was freezing and there was a huge presence surrounding the place. It seemed as though it was in front of the door; but it was also *everywhere*. It kept getting colder and colder. I watched this apparition move toward the hut where Don Lupe was resting and waiting. I don't know what came over me but I jumped to my feet, put my shoes on, wrapped myself in that god-awful blanket, and headed for the front door. My friend asked what I thought I was doing and I heard myself say that I needed to go outside and build a giant fire and perform a sacred ritual while chanting.

The next thing I knew, I was outside chopping wood. It was desolate and cold. I chopped until I had enough wood to build a great fire in the center of the village. When the flames began to grow I declared to the village that the soul of Don Lupe would stay warm tonight and that I would watch over him; I had been chosen. What was I saying? Where was this knowledge coming from? All I knew was that I was being guided. My incantations were similar to a Gregorian chant. I felt as if I was a Native American Medicine Man. As the fire grew larger I began to dance. My terpsichore was of an authentic and genuine nature. I was being allowed to hold space between worlds. The sounds in the village were inhuman and caused a very strange vibration. Then, I am rendered ineffable; I simply have no way of elucidating just how it felt. It was out of this realm.

Don Lupe knew he was being visited. Although I do not know how I knew, I did know that this antediluvian being knew him. It had not yet been decided whether or not he was to live or die. This was indeed an other-worldly meeting.

Now Don Lupe's soul and the fire had become one; and the fire took on a strange and unusual shape. I had to chop wood continuously in order to feed the flames. The little hut where Don Lupe resided seemed as if it were tilted and miniscule. Suddenly, the entity was gone. The fire was red and simultaneously orange. Was that Don Lupe's face in the fire? I felt myself growing weak from the amount of work I was required to do. I had no idea as to what time it must be. All I knew was that I could not stop any of my ritual or Don Lupe may not live.

I was not being fustian, but I knew that the safety of the village was in my hands. I was being allowed to create sacred space and hold that space until this great meeting was finished.

The next visitor seemed sapient and kind. It was as though the moment of truth was upon us: will Don Lupe stay, or is it his time to leave this dimension? I began to increase my work pace. I chopped and chanted and stoked the fire repeatedly at a pace that would make American folk hero John Henry surrender! It was as if the fire was co-mingling with the sky and warming the entire village. This was not only the soul of Don Lupe, but his heart. The love that he had shared with so many was being manifested through the fire. There was a mellifluous tone which seemed to ring out through the land. He was omnipresent. He was being shown his work and the need for him to stay. The village was undulating like the waves in the ocean. Nothing appeared to be solid. I could feel him get stronger as I claimed to myself, "I think he is going to stay!"

I do not remember returning to my little abode. I could feel the presence of Don Lupe's wife standing over me. Night had passed and the sun was quite bright. I was disoriented and hungry and she was tender and kind to me. I could hear the village people gathering. They had not shown themselves until now. Was it all a dream? Where were my friends? How did I get back in here? I thought I might have passed out in front of the fire; I just could not remember. But she knew. She was grateful and lovingly smiled at me while she wept and thanked me in her native tongue. It was then that she beckoned me to come outside into the light. She wanted to prepare some food for me. You see, there was more that was needed. I could not believe the multitude of people; they waved at me as if they knew me while sounding out some kind of a chant of thanks, acceptance, and love.

Casey, a brilliant doctor, walked over to me. She said she thought I might need to sleep for days. I seemed so drained. It was as if my energy had been exsanquinated. Because she is quite perspicacious and keen, it was nugatory to even attempt to convince her that I did not feel as if I had been drug through a key hole. One look at me and her doctor persona was at full mast. Yet, she was busying herself preparing for what was about to happen in the village and she was thriving on the possibilities. She was there to help me with my last task: she knew she had brought me here for a reason and she wanted to make certain that everything was in place. Albeit it seemingly arcane, it was part of a design that Don Lupe had orchestrated.

So perhaps the Dragon represented the Pleroma. What a munificent abundance of energetic stuff. Was this putative for this level of vibration? It began to give me pause. I should already know about this, yet I am in the midst of wonderment myself. It is as though I am moving in slow motion … more than perfunctory, yet I am not certain I am completely in this dimension.

Everyone in the village began to make some indescribable sounds while they beat their chests in a reverent manner. By their gaze, I could tell that Don Lupe was emerging from his abode. It was as though he was a deus ex machine and everyone was awaiting a message from the other world. He was brilliant. He knew what was expected of him and he delivered. How magnificent! He was clearly a hagiographical figure representing the hopes and dreams of this community.

There he was with his signature straw bandana. Although he was frail in body, he was immense in spirit, and they all loved him. As he waved to each and every person there, acknowledging their love and respect, our eyes met. He acknowledged me quietly, in his own special way. By his demeanor he was letting the village know that he trusted me enough to submit to more treatment, and that it was important for all to be present today.

Casey and I began gathering large stones in order to create a sacred healing circle that he would sit in so that I could do one last thing. When the stones were in position, he took a seat in a folding chair in the middle of the circle. Before I put the last stone in place to close the circle, I asked for his permission to join him in the circle. He nodded, I closed the circle, and the event began. We all felt it: something incredible was about to happen. The sun shone on him and it was as if the sky decided to open a door right over him. I told him that the circle extended into the sky and beneath the earth. Nothing could permeate this sacred circle. He smiled and leaned back in his chair while extending his arms out and letting the sunlight beam down on his heart. His heart and the hearts of every member of the tribe were one at this point. It was a fascinating light show manifesting itself all around the village. He was no longer a solid being: he was a frequency and vibration that manifested a special love and joy. I wanted to shout like one does in a Pentecostal church ceremony. Our spirits were quickened and we all knew each other. It was then that I heard the powerful wings of a Dragon … or *something*.

He was no longer an old man. He was timeless and his eyes were drinking the world. I could not stop looking at him in utter amazement. I believe he was actually orchestrating this event, and I was merely there as one of the props. I placed my hands on him while focusing my eyes on something sparkling in the sky. I felt the earth move and time itself changed. There were a myriad of colors everywhere I looked. He and I were just pure energy for about a split second and that is when it happened: I witnessed him heal. I saw the power return to him. It was as though I was seeing it all in slow motion, yet sensing we were moving at light speed. I had no language for what I was seeing. I just knew it was sent and I was being allowed to hold a sacred space. Any moment I expected lift off. Where was that shrill sound coming from? Was that me? Once again, I could see past, present, and future simultaneously. I was no longer standing in the Creatura. This was something else; something I could not describe. When I tried to make sense of what I was seeing it would vanish. I could only hold it in a special state of being. Could this be what the theory of transubstantiation is all about? I know this place. How beautiful and yet so simple it is. I think this is where one sees the face of the Ultimate of Ultimate Concerns. Yet, I cannot describe any of it.

When I came to my senses, the villagers were waving and shouting in a jubilant fashion. There was so much joy and happiness. My friend was standing nearby at peace. It was as though we had witnessed a birth for the first time ever. There was love pouring from everywhere. I could see myself for the first time. All of us viewed everything with awe. That is why I could hardly believe it later when Casey told me I had spent more than three or four hours in that circle. It felt like a second had ticked away. I have longed for that space since … for when in it ... I remember!

Don Lupe stood up and floated toward the crowd. His arms were out stretched and loving, and his face had a warm smile that identified each and every one of us as his loved one. I felt embraced by a heavenly figure. There were hues of green around everything. There was Don Lupe, and all of us. Everyone was energy and there was no separation. I felt the death of my persona adaptation. The new Kurt saw himself unfold and the joy was unimaginable. I could feel them all and they could feel me. Don Lupe was the conductor of this great orchestra. These instruments were magnificent. We were standing in a sublime richness and knowledge beyond that which Earth could offer. Could this be what death feels like … or is this the truth about life? It really is glorious. I understood for the first time why the term "I AM" had been given to Moses. I understood a great deal; however, even as a sesquipedalian I have no words to express what it was truly like.

I felt my body give as though I was releasing every tension I have ever felt in my lifetime. I knew why we breathe. I was standing in spirit's own kaleidoscope. A marvelous being was turning the apparatus so that I could see all the pretty colors. Unbelievable! Wait—there is no separation between life and death. There seems to be some sort of harmonious vibration that if we try to understand, we separate ourselves. Why am I crying and laughing at the same time? I think I started to jump and shout. Oh my goodness! Shakespeare was right, "there is nothing either good or bad, but thinking makes it so." I kept saying that as I explored nothingness. I am love, therefore I deserve love unconditionally. I got it! All I have to do is ask and listen and it will be revealed to me. I just have to move past my ego.

This celebration of life continued for hours. Then we knew it was time to return to our agreed-upon form. It was time to materialize again. The trick was not to forget. However, I was experiencing a conflict of entelechy. I know full actualization is here because I saw it; yet, where did it go? I have to imagine it back into the physical world; I have to hold a space for its rebirth. It exists if I stay focused. Now I am beginning to understand what holding space is all about. Oh my goodness! I am coming apart. I feel myself forgetting. No Kurt—don't let fear enter into your space. I am separating again. No!

I had become dehydrated and needed to be helped back to the hut. Casey was exhausted as well. I do not remember much after that. The village had its ritual leader back and he had his village. I think Casey and I just sat in disbelief for awhile before I just succumbed to my weariness. My dreams were those that you cannot tell if they are really happening. I think this is how we return to the place I was talking about before. This is how we can reconnect with the Pleroma. This is a world of endless symbols that have meanings beyond our dimension. Perhaps it is my a priori that understands it all. I feel autistic, and I am frustrated when I try to tell another.

Could it be that I really cannot tell another? Must they experience this realm for themselves? Is this why Don Lupe will only nod at those who know? I felt the deep silence become a part of my dream. Oh! So the good teacher brings this knowledge out of the student when he or she is ready. Galileo was right: he had to have seen all of this as well. Wait a minute, I think I am dreaming! I think I feel my purpose calling me back into a reality that I designed ... I designed ... I designed.

I did not stay asleep: I woke up sometime much later in the night. I knew that this was my last day there, and a sadness came over me. It was as if I was leaving old friends that I would never see again. I discussed it with Casey and, although she felt the same, she reminded me that she had visited these people many times. In fact, she was helping one of the little village girls get through school.

Although this primitive village was dark by the time this little girl would get home from school, she would gather her books and lessons each night and place them under the only light available in the area. Upon seeing her, I remember just staring because of her commitment to education. You see, her unspoken mission was that she wanted to return to this impecunious area one day and help her people. Even though she was only 10 years old, she had the fortitude of a wise old woman. She would get up very early each morning and wash the only blouse she owned and wear that damp thing to class each day. My heart reached out to her as I observed this kind of dedication to a mission. It made me feel otiose. I was ashamed for the times I complained about a bus taking too long in the city. This little girl was focused and so full of joy; she just felt she had it to do. No problem. Believe me when I tell you that this young girl is destined for greatness. There was a village beauty about her that was so natural.

Later that night, the woman who had been playing music and singing each night decided to pay us a visit. She came into our abode and asked for help. She was confused and distraught because she had felt she would be able to learn the ways of Don Lupe. She had been misinformed by her instructor. She was out of her element and was certainly unaware of the potential danger she could be in by staying there alone in a tent. I advised her to go home. I offered her my services by giving her my phone number and address back in the states. This did not seem good enough and she was angry and disappointed. There was a great deal of hurt in her eyes and pain in her posture. I felt I had let her down. I learned that very evening that we cannot be everyone's healer. For me, I had to stay focused on my assignment at hand; even though my rescue fantasy was raging.

As the night continued to make its presence known, I could hear the sound of silence screaming itself into existence. It was an evening of rapture. My spirit was aware of the very essence of life. I was alive for the first time. Yet, I was rendered ineffable. "No, don't try to analyze it. Just allow yourself to be a part of it." It felt much like wakeful dreaming ... or had I transcended my body? I was at peace with life. I could feel the power of the Pleroma. Why is the sun coming up? Some of it might have been a notion of force that Hegel talks about.

As we gathered our things and prepared to exit this abode, I must admit the space felt warm and loving. There was a kind of transubstantiation and I didn't recognize the space anymore. It had taken on a different energy; it had protected us. I could tell that Casey felt the same; her movements were methodical and precise as if she were practicing her Tai Chi. It felt like we had been in a story and now we were experiencing the denouement.

As I reflect on that special moment, I can only think of Hegel's explanation of the notion of force. To this day I am rendered ineffable. The closest I can get to an understanding would be to share this data from his book, *Phenomenology of Spirit*. In it he states:

> The *Notion* of Force rather preserves itself as the *essence* in its very *actuality*; Force, as *actual*, exists simply and solely in its *expression*, which at the same time is nothing else than a supersession of itself. This *actual* Force, when thought of as free from its expression and as being for itself, is Force driven back into itself; but in fact this determinateness, as we have found, is itself only a moment of Force's expression. Thus the truth of Force remains only the thought of it; the moments of its actuality,

their substances and their movement, collapse unresistingly into an undifferentiated unity, a unity which is not Force driven back into itself (for this is itself only such a moment), but is its *Notion qua Notion*. Thus the realization of Force is at the same time the loss of reality; in that realization it has really become something quite different, viz. this *universality*, which the Understanding knows at the outset, or immediately, to be its essence and which also proves itself to be such in the supposed reality of Force, in the actual substances (86).

He continues:

In so far as we regard the *first* universal as the Understanding's *Notion* in which Force is not yet *for itself*, the second is now Force's *essence* as it exhibits itself in and for itself. Or, conversely, if we regard the first universal as the *Immediate*, which was supposed to be an *actual* object for consciousness, then this second is determined as the *negative* of Force that is objective to sense; it is Force in the form of its true essence in which it exists only as an *object for the Understanding*. The first universal would be Force driven back into itself, or Force as Substance; the second, however, is the *inner being* of things *qua* inner, which is the same as the Notion of Force *qua* Notion.

This true essence of Things has now the character of not being immediately for consciousness; on the contrary, consciousness has a mediated relation to the inner being and, as the Understanding, *looks through this mediating play of Forces into the true background of the Things*. The middle term which unites the two extremes, the Understanding and the inner world,

70

is the developed *being* of Force which, for the Understanding itself, is henceforth only a vanishing. This 'being' is therefore called *appearance*; for we call *being* that is directly and in its own self a *non-being* a surface show. But it is not merely a surface show; it is appearance, a *totality* of show. This *totality*, as totality or as a *universal*, is what constitutes the inner [of Things], the play of Forces as a reflection of the inner into itself (86-87).

On page 99 of his book, *Dreams: God's Forgotten Language,* John Sanford writes brilliantly about the nature and structure of Jungian dreams. He delineates them into nine categories:

- The autonomy of the dream life
- The compensatory nature of dreams
- The significance of dream elements in general
- The significance of certain prominent dream figures
- The dream as a cartoon or parable
- Nonhuman dream symbols, and some rules guiding dream interpretation
- The transpersonal dream source
- Further description of the collective unconscious
- Brief review of the paradoxical nature of the unconscious

He states that in dreams we can meet an unwanted shadow, an alter ego, or autonomous complex. We can be forced to deal with the anima and animus that we are not consciously aware of in our wakeful states of being. Sanford reminds us that consciousness and unconsciousness are always communicating; they just utilize different symbols.

So maybe I was doing lucid dreaming and did not realize it; the mind, really does not make a clear distinction. Maybe this was in between time and space and I am just now coming into a reality that I can language. Oh my goodness, I have no words for any of it. Pleroma!

That is when I could hear the villagers ululating. I could feel them pounding their chests. Don Lupe's smile was radiant, warm, and loving. They were letting me depart without saying goodbye. Instead, they were manifesting gratitude by uttering guttural sounds that expressed the true meaning of the moment. Their tears became my tears. I knew at that point that this was a real experience. This was like listening to a Gregorian chant in a cathedral of some sort. I was embraced by the moment; I knew it was sacred as well. None of the villagers used restraint in their facial grimaces. This was a show of truth in the most extraordinary manner. I was silenced while simultaneously capturing the beauty and magnitude of the moment. This was goodbye, thank you, and I love you encased in one sound. I was mesmerized. The acceptance into their circle was a numinous, primitive ritual that knew the unchartered chambers of my rational mind. This was an antediluvian human bond of love. It was a return to oneness.

I was dazed as I felt the car move down the path away from the village. The three of us stayed silent as we began to recognize our place in the world again. The looks on our faces will remain with me forever. We had defiled time and space in some kind of ancient ritual. There was a slight grin on my face as I wondered if Don Lupe had orchestrated this entire event. Believe me when I tell you that this was an 'event.' Marcel and Badou got it right: we were touched by a pure form of life itself. Yet the event was inchoate. It may never stop unfolding. I felt reborn; but if I am reborn, then I had to have died. Was I instrumental in saving Don Lupe's life or was I initiated? I could hear his laughter as I got farther and farther away.

72

I couldn't stop hearing the music of my thoughts as my memories did a terpsichorean movement through my brain. The history of my existence had been alerted and I knew I would be engaged shortly on a quest deep within my ontological anxiety. I could avoid it no longer—I knew that the captains of my formation were about to present themselves yet again.

These are the wounds that torment me when they begin to bleed. No matter how hard I try, there is no succedaneous replacement for the agony I feel when they come to council. The mulct they bring forces me to kneel in order to ask God for forgiveness. Their blatant messages prevent me from being grandiose. The realities of my transgressions haunt me. There is no peace. Thus, I cannot wander in the arena where ludic fallacy is acceptable. Authenticity is my only solace. The wounds have a place in my life…I use them as radar for the wounds of others. I can identify the wounds of others because I know my own. Maybe one day they will let me sleep.

Since my wounds seem to be sine qua non to my healing process, I suppose it is time to introduce them. Oh yes, they were in the village with me throughout the ordeal. Their commentaries whirled around me like the susurrations of an elder wind. I could not escape then and I haven't escaped now. The mephitic memories of my past stink like rotten meat. Paul Tillich, in his book *The Courage to Be*, talks about having the courage to continue living in the face of hopeless hope. I learned in the village that I had the courage to be, in spite of my wounds.

> "Neurosis is the way of avoiding nonbeing
> by avoiding being."
>
> ~ Paul Tillich

THE THREE WOUNDS

"I onward go, I stop,
With hinged knees and steady hand to dress wounds,
I am firm with each, the pangs are sharp yet unavoidable,
One turns to me his appealing eyes—poor boy!
I never knew you,
yet I think I could not refuse this moment to die for you,
if that would save you."

~ Walt Whitman

***

First Wound

This is probably one of the most difficult things I have ever
had to write. This, for me, is indeed a form of anamnesis.
The action of putting this to paper has coerced me to recall
an event in my life that was life altering. It changed the way
I viewed adults and the way that I would continue to see
myself. It also made me rethink just how I feel about
filiopietistic beliefs and practices. Yet, I did not realize this
until I began to ponder just how devastating it was; and
how it impacted my life.

When I was a young boy, our next-door neighbor had
humbly and respectfully asked my parents if they would
mind if his family kept a chicken coop in the back area of
their yard (it was not allowed because we lived in the
Atlanta-proper area of Georgia). However, our families
were quite close and there were free breakfast eggs
involved. They had also agreed to place the coop in an area
that would be obscured. It was never a problem and they
were lovely people.

75

At seven years of age, I remember being fascinated by this animal community. The rooster really did prance as though he was royalty, and the hens made certain that they performed well for him. You could see their patriarchal society at work. I was just amazed by the way these animals moved and sounded. I remember sharing with my older brother the personality traits that I had attributed to many of them.

Although eventually there were four of us (three boys and a wonderful little girl), at this juncture in my life there were just us boys. My one brother, who is 13 months older than me, was my mother's favorite because he demonstrated a proclivity for intellectualism. He loved to read at a very young age and definitely seemed to be a child prodigy. My mother promulgated this fact all over the known world, and although it is rather amusing now, it didn't feel quite the same then.

Being the number-two child, I took a different path. I was rather rambunctious. I was more curious than Curious George. I seemed to be recalcitrant about blindly obeying the rules and regulations without some sort of explanation. You can imagine how well that went with parents of my generation. Their parents had survived the great depression and they believed that a child should obey without question. I simply had a different philosophy. Some might call my behavior contumacious. I was just a mischievous little fellow with lots of questions about the world and the way it was structured.

My younger brother was adored by my father. His sobriquet was "king." Sometimes he would make my older brother and I treat him as such. If his displeasure was expressed by ululation, it could mean our decapitation. There were some gestures of obeisance required to manifest our respect for his station. Actually, my father was elated that his complexion was lighter than ours. Nonetheless, I loved my little brother. I knew that he was not aware of what my father was doing; he was an innocent child. His station, though, presented great fear and concern for those of us who were deemed lowly servants.

I learned at a very early age that being different could prove to be unsafe. I realized that I was in the middle of a family dynamic that did not allow for rebels. I always saw things differently. Maybe I was channeling from the prelapsarian time period. I just knew that there was more to an equation than met the eye. I was obdurate toward anyone who insisted upon blind obedience. I was also pugnacious. It makes me smile when I think of myself so young, yet so willing to stand up and fight for what I believed. It didn't matter how old someone was. Verisimilitude was my quest. Even then I knew I wanted to do the truth in love.

Our neighbor came to the back fence one summer day to offer my father four of his chickens. He said that they would make great food. He felt that we should experience farm-fresh meat instead of the store-bought variety that we had become accustomed to eating. Of course my father accepted and could not wait to prepare them for dinner. I remember being confused about what that meant. However, I soon found out as I watched my father raise the largest butcher's knife I had ever seen into the sunlight. I was blinded by the sunlight's reflection from the blade. The chicken was making a strange verbal sound. There was fear in the air in a manner I had not heard before. Something was wrong. I use to enjoy knowing we were going to have fried chicken for dinner. But not today! Today I was going to meet death. It was horrible. I remember hearing the horror come from that animal as its head was sliced from its body. When the head hit the ground the torso began to run around the backyard. I remember stumbling backwards in shock. Is this how I get food? There was blood everywhere.

I remember how strong my father's hand looked wrapped around the handle of the knife. He never put it down. He was not bothered by this action. It was necessary. I can still hear the silence. The three of us just stood there as though we had participated in a negative mob action of some kind. Why didn't I stop him?

I don't remember just why my father was perturbed the next day. I do remember that when he came out into the yard he was not happy with my older brother and me. He told us that if there was one more argument there would be a price to pay. He was quite resolute. I had seen this face of confused justice before and I knew he was serious.

All I remember when the bike my brother and I were sharing fell was that the back wheel was spinning. I was mesmerized by it. So much so that I did not realize my brother was protesting loudly. He was blaming me for the crash that had just taken place. I was just fixed on that wheel. It was silver in the middle and the tire was black. The bike was orange and it was fast. I was not really listening to my brother's shouting until I felt my shoulder ache from the way my father squeezed it as he yanked me away from the bike. He inculcated that he had warned me and now I had to be punished severely. I kept trying to tell him it was not my fault. He would not listen. My sentence was already in place. My father would act as the executioner. I saw the large butcher knife raised high above my head. My father had, in prior instances, threatened to cut our heads off. This time he was serious. I remembered the chicken as I felt the blade find its way across my head from ear to ear. I could smell my own blood and felt my body give. Is this what death feels like?

Suddenly my father realized that he had just cut his own son. He lifted me and wrapped my head immediately while he called for my mother. She took one look at me and began to cry. It was as if she were saying goodbye to me. When Dad placed me in the car with my head on his lap I lost track of time. All I remember is being in the hospital undergoing more pain. The doctors were sewing my head. My eyes were covered. I was weak and tired. I felt little. Then I heard one of the doctors ask my father how this happened.

My father taught me that adults were capable of lying that day. He replied that I had fallen from a swing and cut myself on one of the seats. Everyone seemed to accept that story. I just kept quiet and wondered why my dad felt he had to lie.

When I returned home I saw my older brother on his knees praying for me. He was in our room. His eyes were filled with tears. He had no idea my father was going to harm me in that manner. The guilt he felt is still with him to this day, which is more than five decades later. He was just a boy. It was just sibling rivalry. It was natural for brothers to disagree. It was not natural for a young boy to witness his brother's head being cut off because of a spat.

This event has obviously stayed with me. My first meeting with death was not a pleasant one. I was a victim of injustice and I learned that a lie could save you from getting in trouble. It was as though I was suspended in a caliginous space when I heard that lie. It echoed in my ears over and over again.

My father never apologized for that day. We just continued as a family as though it never happened. He never threatened us that way again. He never killed any more chickens either. Interesting!

For years I heard myself lie. I became quite good at it. It became a game for me. Thus, I was brilliant in corporate America. I didn't have a great deal of respect for authority figures. They were scared just like me. I know this because they lied to get out of trouble. They problem solved by using force and violence, and displayed angry faces when they felt they were right.

I remember pondering the story of Abraham and his son. He was willing to sacrifice his son for a greater good. He was willing to participate in a blind obedience; even if it meant his son's life. So, I began to treat myself the way I had been treated. I would sacrifice myself for a greater good. In some cases I would just sacrifice myself. Was I a hero or a victim? Of course, I did not have such clarity when I was younger. I knew the world I was forced to live in was full of deception. I saw what happened to a poor defenseless creature when I didn't voice my disapproval. I learned that I could survive.

Although I didn't think about this occurrence for years, I watched my form take shape around it. This nascent being was born that day: one who knew he had a purpose. He also knew that he could no longer be silent while others were hurt and that he would never be unjustly accused again without being cognizant. He would no longer allow himself to be harmed by a false justice and he applied that to everyone he knew.

Perhaps this was also a beginning of my sacerdotal nature. I did not grow up to handle things like my father. In fact, I find myself kind and gentle in my dealings with people. I can be austere and just; however, violence is not a first resort for me. I am erudite and I do all that I can to do the truth in love. I am powerful and strong, but accepting of anyone who may seem different. I know what it feels like to be different and what that can lead to in a dangerous world.

Second Wound

It was the summer of 1971. I was 22 years of age and had graduated from Xavier University of Louisiana in May. I had returned to Atlanta and was residing with my mother as I awaited the results of one of the most important interviews of my young life: I had been granted a screen test with WSB TV, Channel 2, in Atlanta. One of the news reporters there at the station had sponsored me and felt I had a chance to be the first African American to be accepted to the news team. The station warned me that it would probably take awhile before they reached a decision. So, in the meantime, I needed to find some temporary work.

A family friend had started a horticulture business and needed an able-bodied hand to assist him and his son five days a week. The work was hard and it was very hot that summer. Each evening, when I returned from my temporary work, I would check the mail with incredible anticipation. Even though I knew I would be accepted, I continued to work hard for Mr. Wilson in order to earn my room and board at home. Mom was a single mother with two more children to help through college. She could not afford to just let me sit around the house and wait. I had to make certain I was not costing the household more than she could afford.

Some days, while I would be mowing lawns and pulling weeds, I would just dream of what these home owners would say when they turned their sets on and realized that the on-screen television personality had, at one time, cut and cleaned their lawns! This was truly ritual humiliation; and, at the same time, it was good clean purging work. It was in many ways cathartic.

I had a very dear childhood friend who had finished his undergraduate degree a year before I did. He would come over most evenings, as anxious as I was, to find out about the job offer. We would pretend I was already there and laugh and joke about the impact my debut would have on the city. I loved this man. We had known each other since elementary school and we belonged to a singing group called the El Commodores. My brother and he were the lead singers. I was part of the do-whop background. Those were the days. We were quite good and received a great deal of notoriety for our performances.

I remember the first time we ever performed in front of a White crowd. It was in Carolina. We were at a Catholic summer camp named "Our Lady of the Hills." One of the nuns from our high school, who had accompanied the co-ed group from Drexel High to this camp, was recalcitrant about the El Commodores performing because she did not wish for us to draw unfavorable attention from the Whites. These were racist times. She expressed her resistance to the priest in charge and he vehemently disagreed. We were going to perform!

We didn't have caracas, but it certainly sounded as if we did: our knees were knocking like never before! The nun reminded us before we stepped out on stage not to embarrass the school. Great support!

Then it happened: we started to harmonize in ways you could only expect from the Temptations from Motown records. Everything was just in flow. The mellifluous tones that poured from us were just perfect. Our terpsichorean choreographed moves were especially good that day. You see, we had never heard anyone scream or shout in ecstasy because they loved our sound, so when this happened, we thought we had failed and they were yelling in disgust. That is until we heard, "We love you El Commodores." I will never forget that night.

Kenny Rogers (not the Country Music performer) was the lead singer along with my brother, Andrew. Those were amazing times. I shall never forget them. In fact, whenever we would see each other during school breaks for college we would always get together and hum a few bars. We just loved each other.

So you see, Kenny and I had a rich history together. He was more like my brother than my friend. We shared many confidences. He would encourage me when I was uncertain. He was always there for me. Sometimes, to my amazement, it seemed as if he would speak of me in a hagiographical manner when he told of some of our adventures.

I remember a previous summer when Kenny and I got jobs doing day labor. We needed money for a night out on the town! The jeremiad that I had to listen to from Kenny almost drove me crazy, but we got that awful warehouse job done. We were tired and dirty and it was extremely hot. The foreman was obnoxious and gruff. Glad we chose college!

Kenny knew there was a great deal of bellicosity in my household between my mother and me. He would make certain he would come by each evening to rescue me. Mom and I just did not get along. I was not her favorite. I really wasn't contumacious. I just felt my mother—well, there was a great deal of drinking and mom housed a lot of anger in those days.

It was the summer of 1971 and the whole world was mine. Kenny had started to take karate classes at some center. He was so self conscious about his height. If Kenny were five feet he would be happy! Yet, he was as talented as Sammy Davis, Jr. What star quality this man had!

He told me that he was upset because he was at a party with some of our old friends and some thugs walked in uninvited. They were a motley bunch and they crashed the scene in order to make trouble. The woman sitting next to Kenny said, "I wish a man were here to protect us." Kenny felt inadequate and vowed that he would never have to endure a comment such as that again. So, he decided to become a black belt in karate. Albeit he was quite committed to his practices, he realized this process was going to take longer than it did on some of the television shows. He wanted to be a hero and he wanted it now.

One day that summer, I was in a hurry because I had somewhere I was supposed to be in less than an hour. I had to take a shower, change out of my dirty work clothes, and make a better sartorial statement. I was excited because the person I worked for had loaned me one of his old cars. I had transportation and I couldn't wait to leave my house and spend some of the money I had made. I think I was going to take my younger brother along with me.

I will never forget how I was rushing around the house and, as usual, it was excessively hot. I even knew what station I was going to listen to as I cruised down Peachtree Street on my way to the Fox Theatre to see a movie. I was in a frenzy because I could not find the car keys. I knew I had placed them in a special spot. However, they were not there. Just as I was about to look in yet another room the doorbell rang. I really was not expecting anyone. Who could this be? Well, it was Kenny.

"Kenny, I can't stop right now, I am headed out the door just as soon as I find my car keys." Kenny noticed that I was having difficulty and said he would help me look while he told me about his dilemma. We looked everywhere. Finally, Kenny suggested that we just sit down in the living room and drink something cool and confabulate about his plight. "When you settle down you will see them staring you right in the face."

Kenny told me that he had been asked to spar with one of the other students at his school. There was a belt ranking in question. He was afraid because he did not feel he had learned enough and he did not wish to be humiliated. Kenny was the only Black in the school and he wanted me to help train him for the match he had in four days. Naturally, he didn't want to get hurt. He was desperate and he had always been there for me.

At first I told him "no," that I just didn't have the time. "Besides, just decline and do it later." He looked at me with such disappointment; I had let him down. So, when I got up from my chair, realized that I was not going to find those keys, and therefore couldn't do what I had set out to do, I decided I might as well help a dear friend. He was ecstatic.

There was a large area of grassy land on the side of my house that was part of my mother's property. We gave many parties out there. My father had planted numerous flowers and shrubs. It was a beautiful square of land. My, what wonderful memories are associated with that area. After changing into some gym clothes, I brought Kenny out to that area and asked him to show me what he could do.

He showed me his karate moves and the defense moves they had taught him. He began to demonstrate some of the attacks he learned as well. I observed him the way a coach looks at a potential candidate for a team. Unfortunately, Kenny was horrible. I told him about the training I had received while at Xavier and just how magnificent my instructor was. I shared with him how difficult some of the procedures were. I felt he was being rushed into something he was not ready for at the time. However, he was resolute. He would not back down. He was going to show up with pride. Yes, I had my work cut out for me.

After assisting him on a number of moves and strategies, I told him that he was in trouble. There was just too much to learn and so little time. But, hey, I had an idea: "watch me and mimic what I do."

After about five minutes of hand and leg movements, which really excited Kenny, I wanted to show him something that would save his life if he got into trouble. "Watch this Kenny." I did a hand move and then turned my back on him in order to demonstrate a perfect back kick. It was a movement adumbrated by the distraction of the hands and body motion. Kenny seized the opportunity to show me he could now attack with a hand gesture. However, my leg had already been released. The heel of my foot was true. Kenny walked right into that blow. It felt as if my foot went right through his body. He went down and my world stopped. I lifted him up and in a panic I yelled, "Kenny, you were supposed to be watching!" He was in excruciating pain as he gasped for air. Thank God he was alive. Even though he insisted that he was recuperating, I coerced him to let me take him to a hospital. When we arrived at Holy Family Hospital, I told the doctor what had happened. He was in such pain. They made me wait in the emergency room waiting area until the doctor was done with the examination. When the nurse came out, she looked at me and everything was moving in slow motion. I heard her say as the tears welled up in my eyes, "Your friend will be fine. The doctor feels it is just a strained muscle." I felt my legs give out. I had been so worried. This was more than just a passive fantasy—there was a real possibility that he had been seriously hurt.

I was told I could enter the examination area in order to escort him out of the hospital. Since I had carried him in, I thought there would be no problem in carrying him out. Kenny, on the other hand, felt this was not making him look like the macho man he wanted to be. He was lovingly mad at me for being so nurturing. He could be ornery at times, but he was lovable.

I shall never forget the look on his mother's face when I carried him in the front door. "What have you two been up to now?" she said. She was cooking at the time and moved away from the stove and just looked in the eyes of her beloved son. She gave me instructions: "Kurt, bring him over to his bed and let him get some rest." Kenny's sister, Regina, was there as well. She smiled at me and reminded me just how dramatic Kenny could be at times. Her eyes were kind and loving. We had known each other for years.

Kenny's mother, Mrs. Rogers, insisted on driving me home. She knew that I had driven her son's car to her home. She did not want me to take a bus. She was like a second mother to me. "You boys," she said.

The next day I was working on my job. I was so tired and drained that day. I knew that if Kenny didn't relinquish his spot in this match, I would have to go with him for support. I was so worried and concerned about him. I could hardly concentrate. All sorts of fears danced about my psyche. I could not wait to get home to contact Kenny. He just cannot go through with this. This was a strange day.

1532 Mozley Place never looked so good to me. I walked in the front door and everyone was standing there looking at me. My younger brother placed his hand on my shoulder; and my mother could not find the words she wanted to speak. I sat down at our dining room table, which was a beautiful mahogany table with lions holding the table. All of us did our homework around that table. This is where we shared.

My sister is about nine years younger than me, and she has always been so special and lovely. That day, however, she had a task: her moist eyes found mine as she muttered these words, "Kurt, Kenny died last night from complications from the blow to his stomach. He is dead, Kurt, and I am so sorry." I could see the essence of her being looking at me with the passion of innocent truth. I felt something leave me. "Oh my God, I have killed my best friend!"

The grief and guilt I felt as a result was just overwhelming. There had to be a mountain on my chest. "Oh God, suicide cannot be forbidden in these cases." I hurt in a way I cannot explain. A part of me had died that day and would never return.

The vicissitudes of life can be unkind at times. You see, not long after that event, the people at WSB contacted me to let me know that I was being offered the position. They were jubilant and wanted me to start immediately. I heard myself say that I needed to think about it for a couple of days and then I would give them my answer. I hardly had a speaking voice at that time in my life. Something was not there. The sentence that was constantly being inculcated in my mind was, "If you just knew more you could have saved him." I really just wanted to die.

You guessed it: I turned down the job with WSB. I couldn't face anybody. I didn't want to be seen. I was a murderer. I had killed my best friend. "God, I was trying to save him. I didn't want to hurt him! How could you let this happen?" Instead, I decided to become employed by Hoffman La Roche Laboratories. My life would be changed forever.

It took me 30 years to forgive myself for that tragedy. I finally asked Kenny to let me get a full night sleep. I was standing with another childhood friend, Reginald Lopez, who had stayed by my side throughout the ordeal. Now, some 30 years later he stood with me in front of the grave site so that I could find peace.

I remember some years later, my wife at that time (while in tears) telling me that she felt I had become obsessed with trying to give a life back to the universe. She felt she had married a minister instead of the dynamic actor she once knew and loved in college. I was obsessed. She knew I was suffering. She witnessed the pain, she saw the agony, and she viewed the dark night of my soul. She watched me torture myself each and every chance I got. The sleepless nights were taking a toll on me. I was self-destructive. I should have been in therapy. I just wanted to give back a life. Why didn't I know more?

I decided to make every indefatigable effort to help mankind. "Here, take pieces of me. Won't that do? I don't know how to hurt any worse than I am already hurting. I am numb with pain."

I watched myself move from job to job making every excuse as to why something was not right. I would never be satisfied until I could make sense of my tragedy. I could not drink it away, work it away, or perform enough good deeds. "God, what do you want?"

When I tried to cry, it seemed as though it was lugubrious. Nothing could measure up to a life taken. In order to allay the suffering, I became a voracious reader of self-help books and philosophical works. There must be an answer. The realm of meaningful behavior is merciless.

Am I being too tautological when I keep asking for permission to give a life back? This wound would not stop bleeding. The pain was intense. I could not stop thinking of ad hominems to call myself for not being more careful with a life.

At some point, I had the idea that perhaps I could use that wound to see the wounds of others. "Maybe then I can find some kind of solace in the good work I could do for others." Indubitably, I know what it feels like to hurt at a soul level. This wound has been a great teacher. It has humbled me. "Oh God, listen to your mendicant servant as he offers his wound as guidance for others."

One night I heard my being speak: "Quiet, mind, for it is time for him to do the truth in love." This had to be more than a transcendent function. The healer in me was awakened.

Death be not proud, though some have called thee
mighty and dreadfull, for, thou art not soe,
for, those, whom thou think'st, thou dost overthrow,
die not, poore death, nor yet canst thou kill mee.
From rest and sleepe, which but thy pictures bee,
much pleasure, then from thee,
much more must flow,
and soonest our best men with thee doe goe,
rest of their bones, and soules deliverie.
Thou art slave to fate, chance, kings,
and desperate men,
and dost with poyson, warre, and sicknesse dwell,
and poppie, or charmes can make us sleepe as well,
and better then thy stroake; why swell'st thou then?
One short sleepe past, wee wake eternally,
and death shall be no more; death, thou shalt die.

~ John Donne

***

Third Wound

I start with a prolegomenon because I sincerely
want all to realize that my treatment of this grave
topic of bashing those who are different is not
perfunctory or insignificant for me. I am speaking
from a place of quiet knowledge. When you have
been wounded, you recognize the wounds of others
clearly. You begin to use your wounds as radar to
detect the wounds of your fellow survivors. There is
a sensitive, quiet knowing that lives deep inside
you. But you have to let it speak. You have to learn
to witness so that the language can speak a special
truth and your sensitivities can open a door of love
and support for others. I have this kind of bleeding

91

sight that knows the heart of another. Perhaps this is why I was spared. Maybe this is why death said, "Not just yet, Kurt, I have a task for you in the world."

Once you have been brutally forced out of your body, everything becomes clear. You realize that there is a reality beyond your conscious level. You move beyond ego and you are allowed to see the face of a merciful God. "Oh God, forgive me for my resistance to your call. Forgive me for not moving fast enough. My difference confused me and I wanted to blend in with the oppressors. I danced between the lines so my truth could not be written. I waited to stand up and use my wound. I was once a coward but here I am now Lord—prepared and ready."

His name was Theodore, and he was my first friend in elementary school. "Hello, my name is Theodore, but you can call me Teddy." He had big, beautiful brown eyes and he was as lean as the bean poles in my grandmother's backyard. He was quite fair for a Black boy and he had a distinct way of articulating; he always spoke through a smile. "Say, you want to be friends?"

Teddy was softer than me in many ways. I felt protective of him. He was so very gentle and kind. He was attentive to all. He cried when things hurt. What a concept!

Teddy and I remained friends throughout elementary school and into high school. He actually enrolled in the same Catholic Jesuit Military School that I had decided to matriculate when I was 14.

92

Although Teddy and I were dear friends through high school, it was during high school that his softness and sweetness began to become a topic of discussion. Albeit he was still the Teddy I had always known and loved, he was being treated differently by some of the other students. I watched this brilliant and loving soul start to build a protective wall around himself. It was there but, then again, it wasn't. I had hugged him all my life … why didn't I just hug him out loud, then and there, each and every day? That would have made the statement, "We'll show them Teddy, you have the right to be you." Instead, I showed what a marvelous athlete I was and I became Commander and Chief in the Civil Air Patrol at the school. "Hey, Teddy, how do you like my new armor?"

Teddy joined the Civil Air Patrol with me. He supported me through trials and tribulations. He remained my dear and loyal friend. He demonstrated his courage by being a stable presence in my life. He was there and he knew how to show up well.

We went to different colleges but we stayed in touch. We always saw each other during breaks and spoke of our dreams and desires. Teddy no longer smiled the way he used to. I could see his pain. We had a ritualistic way of bowing our heads and not talking about the elephant in the room. We knew it was there. Teddy needed me to be there for him. He needed me to say I would continue to show up well for him. His closet door was off its hinge; many could see in and were asking, "what kind of clothes are those?" Teddy was always there for me. Where was I for him?

After college, I got a tremendous job with a very large corporation. Slowly, as I began to sequester myself in my success, I moved away from my dear friend. I did it in pieces. I am not certain I was really aware of what I was doing. You see, I had undergone another tragedy in my life and I was numb. Was God trying to tell me something yet again?

One day I got a call from a dear friend, Anita. She was crying because she had just heard. This loquacious and extraordinary woman couldn't even get the words out. She told me that Teddy had died. He died of something that was unusual. It was some sort of virus and it took his life. All she could say was that a school friend with so much love and potential was lying dead in a coffin and that he would never smile with us again.

I was unable to make it to the funeral because I allowed myself to be buried in work-related problems and obligations. Teddy was there for me, but I was not there for him. What a tragedy.

When Anita called to report what had occurred during the wake, she told me about how everyone acted. It was as if Teddy had done something wrong. There was an atmosphere of shame and embarrassment because he had died of AIDS.

A negative ritual was taking place. Former classmates gathered, but did not speak of his special power. Instead, they averted their eyes and spoke of nugatory, feckless topics. Perhaps you are familiar with the negative ritual where everyone gathers but says nothing. "You know, I went to school with him … I didn't know that he…" Then someone says that he or she can't believe he is dead, and then they all just say "yea." You see, it is all about *their* embarrassment and discomfort and not about his loving life. Did anyone ask about his pain and suffering? Did anyone care? I certainly was no help.

And so I confess: "Teddy, I should have been there to act as a ritual leader. I should have poured wine on the floor and spoke of our wonderful celebrations; I should have dropped a petal on the floor for each time you performed a random act of kindness; I should have led our group in a special ritual of dropping a stone in a vase for every time you helped one of us. Each person could have offered an experience with you before they let the stone drop. That would have been a positive ritual. Instead, you received the negative one. You didn't deserve that. You were not this profligate person that got AIDS and died.

"Hey, Teddy, want to be my friend? I am showing up better now. I am speaking up for you now. I can see your beauty through the faces of so many now."

Teddy was there for me, but I was not there for him.

REALIZATION

"Things have their within, I am convinced that the
two points of view require to be brought into union,
and that they soon will unite
in a kind of phenomenology
or generalized physic
in which the internal aspect of things
as well as the external aspect of the world
will be taken into account.
Otherwise, so it seems to me, it is impossible
to cover the totality of the cosmic phenomenon
by one coherent explanation."

~ Pierre Teilhard de Chardin

* * *

"All fixed, fast-frozen relations,
with their train of ancient
and venerable prejudices and opinions,
are swept away,
all new-formed ones become antiquated
before they can ossify.
All that is solid melts into air,
all that is holy is profaned,
and man is at last compelled
to face with sober senses
his real conditions of life,
and his relations with his kind."

~ Karl Marx (on modernity)

Jungian Enantiodromia? Reflecting back on when I was working on Don Lupe for those many hours, and then struggling to find my way to my mephitic, dingy, cold abode; I remember collapsing from exhaustion. As I recall, I didn't awaken until much later that morning. Don Lupe's wife had asked me if I was hungry. When I said "yes," she immediately ordered one of the villagers to prepare me some soup. The familiar sound of a dying chicken returned me to my first meeting with death. For a brief moment, I was lying prostrate in the blood again. "What am I doing here? Is this some sort of trance? Not again!"

The death of that chicken provided the food and nourishment for me and the other villagers who were assisting Don Lupe's wife. Was this some sort of ritual transubstantiation? I was being hurled back into time; I was meeting death again. I was being thrust back through time and made to deal with my wounds. Death has its conditions when you confront it. You have to show up as "the sum total of your experiences." I wanted to just offer what I knew. Ratiocination just won't do. Logic is nugatory. No! At this level of healing, one must enter into the realm holistically. There can be no want of ego. The Self— and only the Self— can engage at this level. This is sacred territory. Death is the whole truth.

In the realm of "meaningful behavior" this chicken's death had purpose and meaning. What a noble reason for a being to die. It was offering me the necessary charge to keep a ritual leader alive so that he could do his work for so many. This chicken was sacrificing its life for the lives of others. What an interesting motif.

Don Lupe's wife was quite aware of my energy shifts. She was more than perspicacious. She was not a foreigner to the numinous world of the unconscious. She was aware of my truth and she could see my struggle. She could smell my fear. The puer had been exposed. The sound of that chicken's throat being cut made me face a deep repressed trauma still lodged inside of me. You cannot lie to your consciousness at this level. All that I am was surfacing, and I could not allow it to distract me. Instead, this wound could also assist me with my knowing.

Another Realization. In retrospect, recall that the moment I arrived at the village, Don Lupe was believed to be out of body. According to Casey he had died. It was at that point that something deep in me began to function; something *beyond* me began to function. My God Self knew what needed to be done. I was truly just a witness. Yes, I could feel the great energy. It was beyond my human condition. I believe it was Zizek, referring to Einstein, who said, "Time is an historical manifestation of existence." I could hear the polemic of Einstein in my head arguing that past, present, and future exist simultaneously. Teilhard de Chardin's concepts of the "phenomenon of man" danced about my thought patterns until I blacked out into my soul. It was there that God could counsel death.

I got it now: my prayer was being answered. "Oh God, please let me give a life back." This mystical/religious experience changed my life forever. It humbled me to my knees. My Self had collided with my ego and I had lived. I had also been instrumental in restoring the life of this very special man.

Years later, as I ponder these events, I wonder, "who was the true healer?" Don Lupe restored me as I restored him. Ah, both are true. My two great wounds were my entrance fees to the great event. I was purged while I was helping another. My ego could not decipher just what had occurred here. Was this why I was chosen? One of my great lessons was that the healer must show up transparent in order to do the great work. There can be no façade. This is how you do the truth in love.

If indeed entelechy is the actualization of form giving cause in contrast with potential existence, then I was allowed to hold a space of magnificent phantasmagoria. Einstein suggests that we must hold our focus and not get distracted so that the magnetic energy can take form and manifest. This was beginning to become clearer to me. I can see it. Stay focused and do not get distracted. The moment you break your focused intention, you have to start over again. "Energy is a constant."

I believe in my heart that something wonderful and inexplicable ignites the energy. Something that Tillich calls the "Ultimate of Ultimate Concerns." Miracles deal with things we cannot explain or even understand with our limited ego. So all we can really do is learn to witness. There is this extraordinary aspect of us that tries to synergistically merge consciousness and unconsciousness. Jung called it the struggle between the Creatura and the Pleroma. There are a plethora of infinite concepts about what it all means. Yet, for me, it is time to just quiet my mind and to witness. Witness!

"Thank you, death, for all that you have taught me." I say this as I again reflect on Donne's poem, "Death be not proud." No, death, you are not my enemy … you are the truth.

THE E-MAIL

"A trauma is an unfinished experience lodged
somewhere in your body."

~ Wilhelm Reich

***

"We are the sum total of our experiences."

~ Socrates

***

"Eternity is neither the intemporal
nor a ceaseless duration,
but rather the profundity of time
construed as an
historical manifestation of existence."

~ Gabriel Marcel

***

It was unusual for my son, Kurt Jr., to contact me in
the middle of the day. I was at work at the time and
sequestered in a plethora of obligations. However,
when the front desk beeped me and said it was my
son, I decided to pick up and tell him I would
contact him later. I knew he would understand
because he knows the nature of my practice. Yet,
this time he hesitated and I could hear in his

breathing pattern the need for him to talk. I could feel myself tense as I waited for his next sentence. His voice seemed strained and weak. He was not as energetic as he is normally. It felt as if the room and everything in it had started to close in on me when he paused and then said, "Dad, I got struck with an accidental blow in karate practice today." It felt as if I was experiencing takotsubocardiomyopathy. Either that or a horse had just kicked me in the chest. All my fears greeted me as I struggled to ask him the nature of his injury and if he were on his way to the hospital.

Rather real or imagined, an acrimonious prediction from Mrs. Rogers was ringing in my ears: "One day you will lose your son." My spirit was already standing in his presence offering whatever aid I could give when I heard him say, "Dad, are you there?" "Yes son, where were you struck?" He told me he had been hit with a round-house kick while he was not ready. It was in the groin area and he was in considerable pain. He told me he was resting at home but that he was experiencing stomach and back pain. I told him that the injury may be worse than he knew, and to call a urologist immediately. I was, of course, prepared to hop on the next flight with all of my healing remedies if need be. Nevertheless, right now, he needed immediate attention. I instructed him to get an ice pack and place it over the bruised area and to promise me he would attend to this immediately. He told me that he would call his doctor and get back to me at once. He insisted that it was not necessary for me to come until he found out more. I reluctantly validated his concern and asked him to keep me posted each and every day until a determination was made. Through remote viewing, I was making every indefatigable attempt to assess his condition. "Dad, let me take care of this," he inculcated. Just before we finished the conversation he relayed to me in passing that he was probably going to test for his black belt sometime in the next week or so. He was disappointed because this injury might interfere with his plans. Then he said goodbye and promised to contact me later. I don't think that what he said really registered because I was so worried and everything in me started to ache. I could hear myself praying, "Oh God, not my son. Not now, death. If you need a life…" Just then I had a devastating memory …

Her name was Tanya and she called me her "Black daddy." You see, she was an Asian American and she had a White daddy, so I could be her Black daddy. She was such a lovely young girl. My family lived on the 21st floor of a high-rise building in Lincoln Park in Chicago and she and her family lived on the 11th floor. She played with my two sons, Kurt and Erik, every day. She would rush home from school just so she could sit and sew and talk to my then-pregnant wife about the baby that was growing inside her. She was so excited. She wanted to have a birth present ready to give to the newly born child when it came. She would laugh and sing with my boys and comb my wife's hair during her visits. She had such an amazing and loving energy about her. What a remarkable being. I remember when I decided to take Tanya, Kurt, and Erik out to the park in order to learn the fundamentals of the game of tennis. The laughter was contagious. I don't know how much instruction I offered that day, but I can tell you we had a wonderful time. She joined us for dinner each and every day. She was truly a part of my family. Her kindness and genuine love were inimitable. When her family would come up to visit with us we would have a feast. This was a time to remember.

One day, right after my daughter had been born, and while performing my executive duties as a VP for a plastic packaging company, I was overcome with the worse feeling. Consequently, I uncharacteristically asked my secretary to cancel my day and I darted for the exit. I had to get home immediately and I could not drive fast enough. It was in the days when cell phones were not prevalent, so I could not just call and double check while in the car. I knew I should have got a car phone but, in those days, cars were being broken into repeatedly just to get the phones. Random thoughts danced through my head as my concern turned to panic.

When I arrived in front of my building there were a number of fire trucks and people in the lobby. I recklessly searched for my loved ones but to no avail. The elevators had been rendered inoperable by order of the fire chief. The doorman said that the chief felt they could contain the fire and that those of us who lived on the floors that were not burning should not really worry. After all, the building was designed so that it could not burn.

I immediately headed for the stairs and ran up 23 smoke-filled flights of them. It was dark and hot and I thought I would collapse at any moment. Yet, my will was greater than my need for rest. My family was up there and I had to get to them. When I finally stumbled to the front door, everyone was scared to death. I had them wrap in wet blankets and told them not to worry we were all going to make it down the way I came up. My wife was incredibly concerned about the baby, "she cannot breathe that much smoke, Kurt." At that point, a big round fireman burst through my front door. He told me that the doorman had told him of my fool-hearty venture. Temerity or not, I could not just leave my family up there alone during a fire. We took a special designated elevator down to the lobby. As I was hugging each and every one of them I asked, "where's Tanya?" My wife told me that she had not come to the apartment that day. That was odd I thought. She never misses a day. She especially makes a point of seeing my baby daughter now. She had waited so patiently.

I can remember the day my daughter was born; Tanya presented her with a stuffed bear that she had sewn. It was just so lovely. My daughter, Kaila, seemed to love it very much. Tanya would hold Kaila and pretend the bear was talking to her. There is nothing more wonderful than to witness the sounds from a happy child.

I don't remember the events exactly, but somehow the doorman and I were on the 11th floor trying to get the door open. You see, I knew she was in there. The black smoke had mixed with chemicals and was strangling us as we tried to kick the door of her apartment open. We almost had it when, suddenly, we got a back draft. Both of us went flying backward. When we realized that we could not do it on our own, we ran downstairs and got the firemen. Everyone kept saying that she was not there, that

Tanya would have run out at the first sign of fire. "She is a smart girl."

I will never forget how Tanya looked wrapped in a blanket and full of soot as the fireman rushed her to the ambulance in order to take her to Children's hospital. Tanya was bloated and disfigured from smoke inhalation. "Bugle Boy" was dead next to her. It seems she had run back to save her cat and was overcome by smoke and flames.

Her parents had left her in the apartment asleep so that they could hurry and buy her Christmas presents. This was a perfect opportunity to purchase all of the items on her list. Besides, she had been rehearsing for the school play and was tired. "Let her sleep."

Her father was not living with her biological mother; however, his girlfriend loved Tanya immensely. They were a special little family and wonderful neighbors. Albeit the biological mother did not live in the building, she did visit from time to time. She was a very special lady. No wonder Tanya was so gifted.

At the very moment the ambulance was about to take off, Tanya's father and his girlfriend returned with bags of gifts in hand. The doorman got to them before I could and they dashed off to the hospital. The building owner invited me to bring my family to her penthouse apartment in the other tower where they would be safe and away from the chaos. It was from there I called the hospital and was told by the girlfriend to please come over immediately. Tanya had died!

When I got there, I was asked to wait in the lobby for just a second. Tanya's biological mother came in approximately at the same time I did. I remember her shaking her head and asking me if I knew what her child had done now. "She probably scraped her finger and her father is overreacting to it or something." I could not let her walk into the room and see her daughter dead with no warning; so, I held her face so that our eyes were locked and I told her that there was a fire at the building and that Tanya had died. I hope I never hear a scream like the one I heard that day. Her ululations were from a place that is reserved for grieving mothers.

When we were brought into the room where the child's body was, her mother began to speak to her. She said, "Tanya, look how stained your clothing is. How did your face get so dirty?" She began to moisten the bottom right side of her blouse so that she could clean her little daughter. Then she climbed on the table, opened her blouse, and pleaded with God to take her soul and give it to her daughter. "Please God, not my child … it really is okay … take mine."

Death had shown up in my life again. I felt so helpless while I tried to console each and every one of them. There is nothing one can say at that point. You can only let them know that they are not alone in their grief. What was I going to tell my children?

There are many events that followed, yet the one thing that reoccurs in my mind is what my son, Erik, said after I told him: "Children aren't supposed to die, right dad?"

If death needed a life, then death could have mine; I was not going to let my son die this way. I was beside myself and hurting in a way I cannot explain. I am rendered ineffable. I was drunk with fear and agony. An old wound had been opened and was exsanguinating the energy from me. Yet, I had to will myself into the treatment room in order to assist a person in pain. That day I really could use my wound as radar for the wound of another.

I stayed in touch with Kurt, and each day he assured me that he was feeling better. Two days had passed and I was beginning to believe him. "Perhaps tonight I can sleep," I thought. My heart had been racing everyday and through each and every phone call. "Please, dad, trust me. I am feeling better."

It was three to four days later when I received an email from a fellow classmate of Kurt's. She was in his karate class. In her email, she emphasized just how spectacular this black belt achievement was for Kurt, and how he had been their inspiration during the four hard years of training. "Sir, I don't know if Kurt has expressed to you just how monumental this is; however, I thought you might want to know so that you could make plans to attend." Somehow I knew I had to be there. It was imperative. I asked the front desk team to book me a flight immediately.

The first thing I wanted Kurt to know was that I was not in Houston to see him get a black belt; I was there to support him no matter what. The black belt would be a bonus. I did not want Kurt to be nervous or to worry about disappointing me if he was not successful. I was cohortative because he is my son and I love him. "Are you well enough for this?"

He was extraordinary. My eyes welled up with tears of pride and joy. He sailed through the air with such authority as he broke wooden boards from all sides of his body. It really was spectacular. It was the second day of a demanding performance. This one was four hours and the one the day before had been equally as long. Yet, he was determined and focused. The visiting masters were quite impressed. I was amazed to witness such dexterity and preciseness. "Kurt, is that you?"

When the test was complete, the Master instructor asked the parents who were present to honor their loved one by placing the belt on them. Since I was the one there, I walked forward. Kurt and I were transfixed in a soulful gaze that transported us to liminal space and time. I could not restrain myself from quivering as the tears of joy and relief took their position in my eyes. As I hugged him I could hear a voice say, "Kurt, it is over. The curse is broken. You have brought honor back to the Hill name in this field." We just held each other and the earth moved.

Kurt continually thanked me for coming to the event. He was moved by my support. All I could say to him was that I wanted to tell him the whole story. "For now, just know that you have broken a curse … the honor is back … and the integrity of the discipline of karate has been reinstated in my household."

Interestingly, just the day before, my son, Erik, had watched his two sons compete for their next-level belt in karate. Can you see it? From my oldest son, to my youngest son, to my grandchildren … there is a flow of honor.

I wish I could just rest from it a while; however, the messages are inchoate. I continually hear myself repeating these words: "Mrs. Rogers, I was trying to help him, not hurt him. My mistake was doing something that I had not earned the right to do." But the guilt is like a constant beat of a drum in my head reminding me that Kenny died because of me.

I learned that there is integrity in teaching. There is a proper stewardship before privilege.

I continually reiterate the warning to my students about hubris and arrogance. Taking short cuts can be deadly. I know.

THOUGHTS

"If I am what I am because you are what you are,
and you are what you are because I am what I am,
then I am not I and you are not you."

~ Hillel

***

"There is nothing either good or bad,
but thinking makes it so."

~ Shakespeare

***

Some time ago, Jane (Brown) Smith, who I affectionately call "Grasshopper," asked me just what I felt the exegetical rationale was in this book. She wanted to know just what specific message I had to share with the world. After ruminating on it for a while, I told her that I wanted to be certain that people understood that healers are people too. It is important to be cognizant of the fact that they must experience the heuristic side of life as well as the empirical. No one is exempt. All of us must learn to survive all aspects of the human experience.

Sharing my wounds, and demonstrating how they helped to transform me, allows others to realize that all of us are part of what Chardin calls "the ineluctable modality of being." As a result, I have learned to utilize my wounds as radar for the wounds of others, therefore assisting me in their treatment. Most of all, my wounds prevent me from becoming grandiose.

By depicting this daedal, mystical landscape I hope I am able to show that there does not have to be a diriment impediment of marriage between the conscious and the unconscious. There is a mystical dialog that allows for both the Creatura and the Pleroma. Sometimes there is no language adequate enough to voice it, but we can witness the space and hold it in our "a priori."

Recently, I was reading Ken Wilber's book, *Sex, Ecology, Spirituality: The Spirit of Evolution*. He opens the second chapter with two quotes (the first is from Immanuel Kant; the next from Georg Hegel):

> Matter, which appears to be merely passive and without form and arrangement, has even in its simplest state an urge to fashion itself by a natural evolution into a more perfect constitution (32).

> God does not remain petrified and dead; the very stones cry out and raise themselves to Spirit (32).

In this chapter, Wilbur was discussing the nature of the pattern, the sciences of wholeness, the dynamic systems theory. As he was developing concepts about a priori reasoning and a posteriori evidence, I could not help but reflect on something that helped me better understand my experience with Don Lupe:

Since reality is not composed of wholes, and since it has no parts—since there are only whole/parts—then this approach undercuts the traditional argument between atomism (all things are fundamentally isolated and individual wholes that interact only by chance) and wholism (all things are merely strands or parts of the larger web or whole). Both of those views are absolutely incorrect. There are no wholes, and there are no parts. There are only whole/parts (35).

Wilbur is referring to something he calls the holons:

There are no things or processes, only holons. Thus, reality is not composed of things or processes; it is not composed of atoms or quarks, it is not composed of wholes nor does it have any parts. Rather, it is composed of whole/parts, or holons (33).

He adds:

As Hegel first put it, and as developmentalists have echoed ever since, each stage is adequate and valuable, but each deeper or higher stage is more adequate and, in that sense only, more valuable (which always means more holistic or capable of a wider response) (21).

Of course, Hegel, Koestler, Eisler, and Wilbur can elucidate these points of physics and metaphysics much better than I can ever hope to offer; however, I have experienced something that took me years to language. I knew it had occurred: I felt my vibration and its frequencies perform a terpsichorean movement through time and space.

My ultimate fear was that I might fractionalize the whole by trying to tell you the part. Can you see my struggle in my quest for verisimilitude? I think I am a victim of cognitive dissonance. Was I some titular healer summoned in order for the story to reveal itself? If my position was sinecure, was I merely a fragment in the gathering toward a whole? I have pondered my role in this process for years, and I still do not know completely what occurred. However, I do think about it.

As I tell this story now, I can think of many exegetical rationales. Have I been arrogant in arriving at the version I share with you? Believe me, I am humbled in the telling. Yet, I think that Don Lupe knew more than he was sharing. Casey kept inculcating that point each and every day. She is an important part of this story. Her expertise and erudition were a great help to me and to all concerned. Having her to confabulate with during this phenomenal process helped me to stay grounded and sane. She is a remarkable healer as well.

Jungian synchronicity was apparent at every turn. There were happenings that presented themselves, without warning, after we had just discussed the possibility of such a dynamic presenting itself. The conscious and unconscious were manifesting in ways that are ineffable. What an encounter.

I love using the quote, "Imagination gives shape, form, and color to unformed mental energy—both positive and negative." You see, Hegel was right about sense certainty. There were times I was not certain whether it was my active imagination, my sense of knowing, or the thing itself that I was experiencing. Yet, I can tell you how it felt; I can share with you the results of my holding a space of witness. Although I saw others see and experience the same things I did, these occurrences were beyond my mental scope. I know that when I speak of death, I visualize the cold, barren abode I shared with him. What a frightful syszgy—death, Don Lupe, and me.

When you experience something of this sort you begin to question reality. As I listened to voices of possibilities sough to the trees, mimicking the wind, I could hear the tones and chords of a forgotten world. The susurrations accompanied these tones as though it were rehearsed beforehand. I knew that it was all much larger than me. I could only feel my way through at this point and utilize my intuition.

Since my head was having difficulty believing what it was seeing, I had to rely on my heart. Hegel says:

> But, in the first instance, *the return of the feeling heart into itself* is to be taken to mean that it has an *actual* existence as an *individual*. It is the *pure heart* which *for us* or *in itself* has found itself and is inwardly satiated, for although for itself in its feeling the essential Being is separated from it, yet this feeling is, in itself, a feeling of *self*; it has felt the object of its pure feeling and

this object is itself. Thus it comes forward here as self-feeling, or as an actual consciousness existing on its own account (132).

As I continue to ponder this "event," as Alain Badiou would suggest, I think about some of the other possible treatments I would have utilized; and I think of the modalities that were developed as a result of this "event" (the "event" meaning the aspects of a kairos, as both Marcel and Badiou refer).

In retrospect, there are a number of modalities I would consider. Remember in the story when I mentioned the guide's experience with the bed moving, and him feeling as though he was being attacked by some entity that was holding him down? Well, due to that event, and others similar to it, I would consider utilizing Energetic Response Therapy (ERT).

ERT is an aspect of Advanced Psychosomatic Character Therapy (APCT) which deals with metempsychosis (transmigration of a soul from one body to another), as well as overwhelming entity integration. This process is aimed at reestablishing the "I AM" as the core signature for one's vibration. Albeit extraction of the undesired energy vibration may be part of the problem, the focus in ERT is on reconnecting to one's Center—where purity of Being lives.

This procedure normally takes three to four treatments depending on the individual. It typically involves a team of practitioners trained in APCT healing methodology. In many circumstances, responses can be immediate. In others, it may take one to four weeks before a clearing is realized.

Since the personality and the essence of Being are not the same, one might experience a more positive shift toward authentic personality after treatment. The client can expect a return to independence and a sense of clarity and connection to his or her Higher Power, allowing for a soulful expression of one's perfect Self—the "I AM."

Note that I am fully aware of Dr. Paul Chambers' elucidation concerning sleep paralysis. He describes a number of incidences in his book, *Sex and the Paranormal*. For example, on page 17, he describes this particular case:

> The following case is a classic example from an interview Hufford did with "Pat" a 24-year-old woman:
>
> "I was in my bed. It was late at night. I was on my back and I heard a snarling sound…whatever it was I thought it was a male. And… I just felt an incredible weight upon my chest as if somebody (had) put a large boulder there…and somebody had their hand up against my throat…and I remember that it was dark and it had red eyes… ."
>
> The following account comes from "Carol," a young student who believed she was residing in a haunted house:
>
> "I was… in bed [and] the light was out in the room, but it was on in the hallway. And the door opened. The

door knob jiggled and I thought it was the wind from the windows... and then the door opened ... and I didn't see anyone come in. But then I looked back at the doorway and there was this bright shimmering substance, you know....like this very vaporous looking thing. And as soon as I saw it I was just scared stiff. Paralyzed! And it just sort of floats over to the foot of the bed. And I heard this 'hhhhhh-hhhhhhh' heavy breathing, and I thought 'Oh my God!' And I'm rationalizing, I'm saying, 'It's a dog! It's a dog! It's me! It's me breathing!' And so I held my breath and the breathing continued. And then it abruptly stopped. And whatever it was come around to the side of the bed and walked behind my back. And I'm straining my eyes to see it, but I can't move my head, because I knew as soon as I did I was just going to be this close to it, and I couldn't stand the thought. Well, I just—I couldn't move!"

Chambers then, on page 21, gives an explanation of sleep paralysis:

The clinical definition of sleep paralysis is of a person who wakes up to find themselves temporarily unable to move any part of their body except the eyes. The person can remain paralyzed from a few seconds to several minutes, and will only be able to move after making an effort to twitch a small muscle. Once this is achieved, the state of paralysis is broken and the person can move once more.

Casey and I were present in the sleeping quarters with the guide during the occurrence of him pointing out this entity coming for his soul. I assure you, this was not sleep paralysis. The guide was moving his body and screaming while he was fully conscious. I was fully awake and there *was* a presence. We witnessed his discomfort, fear, and trauma. This was a paranormal event. Casey is a doctor extraordinaire; and although, at first glance, she thought that it could be a sleep paralysis, as it progressed she knew otherwise. This woman may be a gifted intuitive, but she is a scientist first and foremost.

Seeing this happen before my very eyes changed my life. The guide felt that he was out of integrity with his village and teachings and therefore decided to go on a pilgrimage for expiation. He, as well as Casey and I, were convinced that something had entered into that room. I told my two companions that I had felt that energy before and I thought I knew just what it was. I remember the look on their faces as I turned to an area of the room and asked, "Death, is that you?" Call it active imagination, label it what you want, I got an answer. Death came into our space that night. The guide acknowledged it as well.

Years have passed since my visit to that area of the world; however, I continue to think of these events often. If I had the chance to assist Don Lupe and his villagers again, I would implement an Intense Chakra Cleanse for Don Lupe; and I would do a healing on the villagers by utilizing a Holograph. Because of the mystical landscape in which we were forced to participate, I would place Casey and the guide in an Altered State so that they could glean data from the unconscious and utilize it in their present state of being.

Let me explain what an Intense Chakra Cleanse, Holograph, and Altered State are exactly:

Intense Chakra Cleanse

Chakras are energy centers that are the openings for life energy to flow in and out of our auras. They serve to vitalize the physical body and develop our self-consciousness. Chakras are associated with our physical, mental and emotional interaction. When they are blocked or closed, we function at a lower level than is desirable.

Working with the seven main chakras, the practitioner takes an energetic reading to determine if there is blockage in any particular chakra. He or she looks for specific locations, how deep the blockage may be, and/or whether the blockage has altered the entire system. Equally checked are the vibrational responses to compare them to the client's core vibration. The rate of frequency and vibration of the chakras is measured and established using intuitive, tuning fork, and systems methodologies.

The key to this procedure is precise harmonic balance. When the chakras are properly aligned, and energy is centered in the body (allowing uninterrupted flow of chi), disease cannot take up residence. This two-hour process requires focused vibrations; chakra-specific essential oils; empathic, energetic listening skills; and a specific intention set by the practitioner. Due to the rearrangement of the client's metabolism, he or she is generally in a trance-like state and can be disoriented for 24 hours after the procedure.

Holographs

The Holographic Principle is an idea initially developed in Physics by several important theoretical physicists, including David Bohm and Leonard Susskind (see current developments in Superstring Theory), which in essence states that the universe behaves as an holographic field in space and time (in four or more dimensions depending on the specific theory) where each point contains information of all events from anywhere in space and time. This is an intrinsic characteristic of Holograms in Physics where "the whole is manifested in each part." Curiously, this scientific principle sounds very similar to the concept of Akashic Records from the Hindu tradition, which is said to contain all information, past, present, and future. To avoid confusions, please note that the Holographic Principle and Holography as a photographic technique are two different things, although related by the definition of Hologram (Spiritandscience.org).

In APCT, a hologram treatment consists of the following steps:

1) Ask the individual or group to close their eyes and create a picture of a specific issue, such as

"what is keeping you from moving forward in your life?" (Please note that it is not important for you to know what the image is; in fact, it may be detrimental).

2). Ask the individual or group to intensify the image.

3). Ask the individual to project the image into the space halfway between you (or into the center of the circle with a group).

4). Reach your "knowing" out to meet the energy that has been projected. See it in your mind's eye. Do what needs to be done in order to shift the energy into a more positive aspect (various methods may include pulling out barbs, filling in holes, shifting the shape, and/or adding additional energy in order to "brighten").

5). FOLLOW YOUR INTUITION and complete the work.

6). Ask the individual or group to bring the energy back into themselves.

7). Bring the space back to neutral and ask the individual or group to open their eyes.

Altered States

An altered state of consciousness is any state which is significantly different from a normative waking beta wave state. The expression was coined by Charles Tart and describes induced changes in one's mental state, almost always temporary. A synonymous phrase is 'altered states of awareness.' An associated body of research has been conducted in trance and this is becoming the predominant auspice terminology. Trance includes all "altered states of consciousness" as well as the various forms of waking trance states.

An altered state of consciousness can come about accidentally through, for example, fever, sleep deprivation, starvation, oxygen deprivation, nitrogen narcosis (deep diving), or a traumatic accident.

It can sometimes be reached intentionally by the use of sensory deprivation, isolation tank, or mind-control techniques, hypnosis, meditation, prayer, or disciplines (e.g., Mantra Meditation, Yoga, Sufism or Surat Shabda Yoga).

It is sometimes attained through the ingestion of psychoactive drugs such as alcohol and opiates, or psychoactive plants and chemicals such as LSD, DXM, 2C-I, Peyote, Marijuana,

Mescaline, Salvia Divinorum, MDMA, psychedelic mushrooms, Ayahuasca or Datura (Jimson Weed).

Another effective way to induce an altered state of consciousness is using a variety of Neurotechnology such as Hemi-Sync, psychoacoustics, mind machines, light and sound stimulation, cranial electrotherapy stimulation, and such. These methods attempt to induce specific brainwave patterns, and a particular altered state of consciousness (en.wikipedia.org).

Naturally-occurring altered states of consciousness include dreams, lucid dreams, euphoria, ecstasy, psychosis, as well as purported premonitions, out-of-body experiences, and channeling.

Perhaps this case can demonstrate the power of such a treatment:

Bill was a 52-year-old adult male who had come to see me. He had an advanced degree and a prominent position. He was divorced and had plans to marry a wonderful person in the next few months. This person complimented his academic side, as well as his spiritual quest. Albeit everything finally seemed to be going according to his plan, he was not satisfied. He felt that something was incomplete. He was still searching for peace of soul. He was not yet over his bitter divorce, which caused him an identity crisis. He was angry at a subconscious level, but was virtually unaware of his vitriolic temperament. He felt that the world had dealt him a harsh blow that he did not deserve. Nothing seemed to feel right and his life was full of highs and lows. Even when he smiled, you could see the struggle to convince himself that all was not jejune.

When Bill came to see me, his request was for a past-life regression. I told him that I did not do the standard regression where I simply reviewed a past life. I told him about the Alternate State that I could perform for him in lieu of the simplistic offering that is normally suggested. After listening to a terse elucidation about what to expect, he felt that this was the right thing for him.

Utilizing the format suggested in APCT therapy (see below), I guided him into a deep state of hypnogogic space. I directed him to journey through the colors, space, and time that would present itself in this state of being. He was completely in a trance-like state as he meandered through the corridors of his being. I guided him beyond his present life and as far into the beginning as his being would allow.

Bill began to talk about the pure energy he could feel and see. He had a wonderful awareness of love all around him. He felt he could sense, as Tillich would say, *the Ultimate of Ultimate Concerns*. The meaning of his life started to unfold as it ignored past, present, and future. He could understand the concept of everything existing simultaneously. He began to talk about patterns and focus. He told me about some distractions he had along the way that he had given form. He was basking in his essence and he knew it. He kept saying how confident he felt in this state. He was cognizant of his core.

Bill said that he now knew what an untampered-with soul feels like. He was trying to reach its purest glow. He began to talk about life experiences throughout the centuries. It didn't matter whether he was male or female because he was dealing with a familiar dynamic in each scenario. Everything was becoming clear now. He had been vehement about confirming a world view that he continually used as a leitmotif throughout his existence. He was a theme looking for a form.

Wasn't it Einstein who said that energy is a constant? Form changes, but energy is a constant. Now, because it was all unfolding before him, he didn't have to repeat the pattern anymore. He realized that he was perfectly him. As he unfolded to his perfect self, his purpose would present itself to him.

Bill's body was shifting and contorting as it acknowledged each and every emotion he felt. Again, I think it was Einstein who stated that the body is not a solid but a set of frequencies and vibrations. Well, Bill was vibrating at an advanced level. His body was transforming. He was transcendent, but inclusive, in his renascent splendor. Bill was doing a paradigm shift. He was shedding all of the nugatory aspects of his life and allowing his soul to celebrate. He repeatedly shouted how euphoric he felt in this space. He was aligned with his core and, thus, his a priori was activated.

Realizing that I had held him in this state for at least an hour, I thought it best to return back to his conscious knowing. There is a meticulous process of grounding someone after they have experienced this procedure. So, in an abecedarian manner, I titrated him through the necessary stages until he was safely home.

Bill spent the next hour talking to me about his amazing experience and all that he had witnessed. He felt so confident now about how to organize his life. He knew that he had to change his perspective and allow his higher self to manifest. Somehow everything was clearer. There was so much to process with this new frame of reference. He was munificent. His effulgence was apparent to him as well.

When I felt it was safe for Bill to get up from the treatment table and ready himself for the world outside my office, I reminded him of some key points in his experience and recommended he reflect on them. As he was leaving, he reiterated how magnificent his experience had been and that he could not think of words to thank me. He then said, "There is just one thing…what about my past life?" I remember smiling and saying, "What do you think the very beginning of your being is?"

In APCT, an altered state is induced as follows:

1). Ask the individual to lie down on a table or on the floor.

2). Ask the individual to breathe long, slow, deep breaths in and out (preferably through the nose).

3). Make note of the individual's level of relaxation. When you feel the individual is relaxed, ask him or her to think of a color and then to tell you what that color is.

4). Ask the individual to imagine that color inside of him or herself, within the third eye, as if it was a fog bank.

5). Ask the individual to walk through the color.

6). Check in with the individual: has he or she walked completely through? If so, what is on the other side?

7). Follow the individual's visions: allow him or her to lead you through their vision, and make note of powerful images and ideas.

8). When you feel that you have taken the images as far as possible, bring the individual back to the fog bank of color.

9). Ask the individual to walk back through the fog bank to this plane of existence.

10). You can help facilitate his or her return by asking the individual to breathe energy up into his or her feet, knees, thighs, and so on … up through the body, bringing his or her awareness back to the physical. Ask the client to sense the room and his or her place in it.

11). When you feel he or she is ready, ask the individual to open his or her eyes.

I realize that much of this information was gifted to me after my initiation in the village. I believe that Spirit knew it was safe to reveal more of this kind of phenomenon to me because I had passed the test regarding deep humility in the face of healing. Again, as Fools Crow said, "I am but a hollow bone. The energy flows through me and does what it needs to do. My job is to keep the bone clean."

Albeit I feel that I was being guided by a Divine hand throughout my time in the village, in hindsight I would add a more structured healing format. I had spontaneously reacted to each situation as it burst into action. I had no idea what to expect moment to moment. Yet, I knew exactly what to do. It was as if I was already there waiting for myself to show up. What I was doing was simply how it happened.

I think that when one is called upon to heal another, that person transcends the dimension that is familiar, thus bringing into existence that which has not previously existed in this realm. Ken Wilbur would refer to that as "transcendence but inclusion." For me, entelechy comes to mind. I believe the healer finds a way to hold a magnetic space in order to be a catalyst for actualization. Of course the concept of intention is essential, but the healer must remove him or herself from the formation of the extraordinary or he or she might limit the phantasmagoria. The healer must let life happen to life, and reality to unfold to its own understanding of itself in its many stages of the whole/parts. I learned that the Thaumaturge is an activator and, as a result of this magnificent experience, I realized that I am not always conscious of what I know. Finally I understood the meaning of "let go, let God." It was so much larger than me. I am rendered ineffable.

So the great shaman was spared by death that time; however, death did not leave his side. Instead, it had been peeled off like a desquamated patch of dead skin. Yes, Don Lupe received a reprieve from death that time; however, he and I knew they would meet again after his task was complete.

This adventure taught me a great deal about my vulnerability. I learned that there are great powers in the universe that I should at least respect. I am fully cognizant that without the help of God I am powerless in the face of death. I learned that there is a place that does not need an up or a down, an in or an out, it just is. Humankind creates a reality based on suggestions which stimulate one's imagination and thought process. To stand contumacious in the face of a Collective Unconsciousness requires a great deal of core knowledge of the true self.

It's as though just before we stepped into this reality, something divine said, "find you … because, when you find you … you will see your purpose."

I think I get it now. You are perfectly you. No one can be a better you. When you find you, then your purpose will be there waiting for you. I think to do so you have to be willing to return to neutral. Ah! The Pleroma.

CONCLUSION

"Where the divine supernatural
meets the mystical mind
at the juncture of the marvelous,
Thaumaturgy will inevitably result."

~ Anonymous

***

You are already there waiting for yourself to show up. The process is how it happened and the call is the activation of the language emitted by the Pleroma that takes shape in the Creatura. The active imagination may cause the shape and form of a dragon, but the information is implemented by the unconscious trying to make its presence known in the conscious world.

Thus, a mystical landscape emerges and forms a kaleidoscope of phantasmagorical events. This is a marvelous expression of how knowing is transmitted into the now. It is extraordinary just how animated we become when we are charged with the many possibilities of energetic suggestion. Story is just an attempt at meaning. Yet, the interpretation is not the thing itself; it is merely a part of a whole. Finding the core of the core is more complicated than just looking; it is looking beyond while acknowledging what is, as well as the potential of more.

Creation is fascinating.

The Dragon's call coerces us to allow ourselves to surrender to right action; and it involves more than just entelechy. It allows for an aligning with the Ultimate Truth. Perhaps Claudel got it right when he suggested that we must attempt to return to nothing in order to find our true selves.

Here we can reflect on the writings of Paul Tillich. In his book *Love, Power, and Justice* he states, "Life is being in actuality and love is the moving power of life." He continues, "Power actualizes itself through force and compulsion. But power is neither the one nor the other. It is being, actualizing itself over against the threat of non-being. It uses and abuses compulsion in order to overcome this threat. It uses and abuses force in order to actualize itself" (47). Thus, I think it is important to consider what he felt was force as well. He said, "The term force points both to the strength a thing has in itself and to the way in which it has effects on other things. It forces them into a movement or behavior without using their own active support. Of course, no thing can be forced into something which contradicts its nature" (46).

Don Lupe was an agent of the call. Equally, he understood the potentialities of things which were being altered and moved. He truly was a sui generis in his community. He held a healing space for all who came into his presence. He taught me a great deal about healing without ever elucidating one principle. He was pedantic because he was so willing to share what he could see and not see. His gentle manner was intoxicating; he merged with everything. By simply allowing me the space to bask in the truth, he manifested a sacred moment. He taught me the brilliance of light.

Having this experience has forever changed the way I practice holistic healing. I think of Don Lupe often as the story continues to unfold. You see, I realize it is inchoate. The sublime verisimilitude is advancing into yet another stage of reality.

BIBLIOGRAPHY

Beaulieu, John. *Music and Sound Healing in the Arts.* Barrytown: Stanton Hill Press, 1995.

Bishop, Paul. *Jung's Answer to Job.* New York: Brunner-Routledge, 2002.

Chambers, Paul. *Sex and the Paranormal.* New York: Sterling Publishing Co., Inc., 1999.

Edinger, Edward F. *Science of the Soul, A Jungian Perspective.* Toronto: Inner City Books, 2002.

Hall, Manly P. *The Secret Teachings of All Ages.* New York: The Penguin Group, 2003.

Hegel, Georg. *Phenomenology of Spirit.* Translated by A.V. Miller. Oxford: Oxford University Press, 1977.

Jung, C.G. *Four Archetypes, Mother/Rebirth/Spirit/Trickster.* Princeton: Princeton University Press, 1959.

LeShan, Lawrence. *The World of the Paranormal.* New York: Helios Press, 2004.

McNeill, John T. *Calvin, Institutes of the Christian Religion, Volume 1.* Louisville: The Westminster John Knox Press, 1960.

Moore, Robert L. *The Archetype of Initiation: Sacred Space, Ritual Process, and Personal Transformation.* USA: Xlibris Corporation, 2001.

Moore, Robert L. *Facing the Dragon: Confronting Personal and Spiritual Grandiosity.* Wilmette: Chiron Publications, 2003.

Perry, John Weir, M.D. *The Self in Psychotic Process: Its Symbolization in Schizophrenia.* Berkeley and Los Angeles: University of California Press, 1953.

Sanford, John A. *Dreams: God's Forgotten Language.* New York: HarperCollins, 1989.

Tillich, Paul. *The Courage to Be.* New Haven: Yale University Press, 1952.

Tillich, Paul. *Love, Power, and Justice: Ontological Analyses and Ethical Application.* London: Oxford University Press, 1954.

Wilbur, Ken. *Sex, Ecology, Spirituality: The Spirit of Evolution.* Boston: Shambhala Publications, Inc., 1995.

ABOUT THE AUTHOR

With national and international recognition and acclaim, Kurt Hill is modernity's version of a Thaumaturge. Kurt has been involved in the study and practice of holistic health care for more than 20 years and, during that time, he has created a unique type of healing, which he calls *Advanced Psychosomatic Character Therapy* (APCT). APCT effectively integrates vibrational and energy medicine; Reichian and Neo-Reichian bodywork; therapeutic massage; and spiritual counseling.

In addition to being a Licensed Massage Therapist, Kurt offers CranioSacral Therapy (Upledger Institute, Levels 1 and 2); Trigger Point/Myofascial Therapy; Healing and Chelation Therapy; and Healing Touch. He has studied the practice of dream analysis, with a particular focus on the theories and practices of Jungian analysts: Drs. John Sanford, Robert Johnson, James Hall and Robert L. Moore.

Internationally, Kurt has studied advanced healing techniques in Japan; Holotropic Breathwork with Dr. Stan Grof in Switzerland; and has been exposed to studies in China. In 2011, Kurt graduated with a Masters in Divinity from the Chicago Theological Seminary with a specific focus in the "psychology of theology" and Jungian theory.

Kurt offers seminars and training in APCT (levels 1 through 3); Holotropic Breathwork; psychic phenomenon; electromagnetic readings (and their specific meanings); medical intuition; as well as a wide array of workshops for facilitating personal growth. Past educational offerings have included internship training through the Soma School of Massage Therapy in Chicago, Illinois.

Kurt has three amazing children (now adults): Kurt Jr.; Erik; and Kaila; a wonderful daughter-in-law, Nikki; and four cherished grandchildren, Noah, Jonah, Bella and Lillah. He lives in Chicago with the "love of his life," Sara Davenport.

Made in the USA
Las Vegas, NV
02 February 2022

42862171R00083